# BROKE DOWN CHRISTIANS

*From Confession to Change: The reality of our compromised Christian living*

LASHONDA JEAN-JACQUES

Copyright © 2016 LaShonda Hanna Jean-Jacques

All rights reserved. No part of this publication may be reproduced, stored in a retrieval system, or transmitted, in any form or in any means – be electronic, mechanical, photocopying, recording or otherwise – without prior written permission from the copyright owner.

AMPLIFIED BIBLE (AMP) scriptures taken from © 1987 by The Zondervan Cooperation. Used by permission.

NEW KING JAMES VERSION (NKJV) scriptures are public domain.

NEW LIVING TRANSLATION (NLT) scriptures taken from © 2012 by Zondervan. Used by permission.

ENGLISH STANDARD VERSION (ESV) scriptures are public domain.

Edited by Valentina Facyson & Pastor Allen Chavis

Cover Design by Perie Wolford

ISBN-13: 978-0-692-82011-7 (Paperback)

# ACKNOWLEDGEMENTS

Dear God,

    I am in awe of You oh great I AM. Thank You for letting Your I AM power dwell within me to banish doubt and propel me into purpose. Thank You for Your perfect love casting out all fear in me, and Your radiant light cultivating honesty and obedience. I AM, thank You for being You, forever worthy and lavishing Your unfailing love on my life. Thank You for Your clear instruction for my life in this season, for giving me an occasion to rise to, an opportunity to be better, serve greater and love deeper.

Dear Husband,

    Thank you for holding me accountable, keeping me relatable and never let me wallow in self-doubt regarding this assignment. Thank you for putting up with the lights being on all hours of the night while I typed. Thank you for taking the baby and giving me peace and quiet to focus and finish even though you were injured and exhausted. Thank you for gracing me, praying with me and keeping me laughing through every good and bad day. Thank you for listening to me go on and on about ideas and thoughts. Babe, thank you for inspiring integrity.

Dear Reader,

    This book is for your Christian self! You are loved, beautiful, amazing, and so precious. Thank you for reading, and thank you for letting your guard down long enough to receive this message. God is forever mindful of you and His love stands as an impregnable fortress for every area of your life, your past, present and future.

Dear Baby Boy,

As your due date grew closer and closer, I searched within myself for all the wisdom I wanted to share with you. I searched for something to give you throughout the years of your life. I thought, I should tell you to be all that you can be in Christ, to pour out your life in service to others with your purpose, to love God and others extravagantly. But as I found these desires, I also found one harsh reality, I could not offer you the best gift of all, an example. You see, if I did not complete this book, a privileged assignment from God Almighty, how could I expect you to find any truth or comfort in my words about your future and potential? Baby boy, when this book is published you will be six months old, and I want you to know that you reignited your mother's sense of urgency about God's work. One day, I will do the same for you. Thank you for inspiring faithfulness in me.

Dear Family,

To my earthy fathers John Caley Sr., Errol Pitterson, and Michael Minns, thank you for all that you have been to me and given me, especially for the example. To beloved aunts Pachridee, Stephanie, Connie and Karen, thank you for being examples of what it means to be a Proverbs 31 woman, for outgiving yourself every day and letting your light shine so that I might see and glorify God in heaven. To my sisters, thank you for being a sounding board, my diary, my shoulders and for keeping me grounded.

Dear Investors,

Church family in the Bahamas and US, thank you for watching for my soul, for your intercessory prayer and your correction. Close friends who loaned me your parents, who invited me into your homes, thank you for sheltering this destiny. To my teachers and mentors who dragged potential and maturity out of me, thank you so much for your tough love, coaching and cheerleading.

# CONTENTS

PRELUDE

PRAYER

### SECTION 1: BROKE DOWN SELF

Snapshots & Selfies

Shame

Chamber of Secrets

Prayer

Unworthy

### SECTION 2: BROKE DOWN NEIGHBORING

Loving My Neighbor as Myself

Don't Watch Me Die

Do Unto Others… Because It's Unto Christ

Prayer

Self-Love + Loving Others

Jealousy & Envious Love

I'm in my Feelings

Sandpaper

Modern Day Pharisee in Me?

Don't Count Me Out!

Journal Entry: Self-righteousness & Self-Serving

Prayer

## SECTION 3: BROKE DOWN HEART

Heart Matters

Prayer

Belief

Surrender

Prayer

Tune Out to Tune In

Prayer

Dull Weaponry

Prayer

## SECTION 4: BROKE DOWN PURSUIT

The Rough Side of the Mountain

Prayer

Too Much Wait

Prayer

Journal Entry: Procrastination

Prayer

## SECTION 5: BROKE DOWN CONVICTION

Only God Can Judge Me!

The Prophet, the PropheLIAR, & You

Journal Entry: A Heart to Obey

God Broke My Heart

## SECTION 6: UNBROKEN

Journal Entry: Redeemed

Come as You Are

# PRELUDE

When I was a child, my mother would buy me a new pair of earrings and a watch almost every year because I always seemed to lose them. Accented by our beautiful Bahamian dialect she would say, "Shonda you can't keep nuttin' man. You gatta learn how to keep valuable stuff." Truth be told, it took me a long time to learn how not to lose my jewelry. So you can imagine my profound shock that God – GOD trusts me to write a book. This book is like me learning to keep my jewelry, it represents me learning that there is a deeper purpose for my relationship with God other than just me getting to heaven. I know that this book is a means to store up treasures in heaven, a means to reach the nations for Christ, a means to demonstrate I love Him with my time, resources, mind, soul, and strength.

This book is written first to myself, it is my personal breaking and practice in discipline and obedience, my personal expression of love to God. It is my personal way of pouring out this area of my life as an offering to Christ. Even so, this book is also written to you and for you. Yes, you, the one struggling to maintain your passion for Jesus. You, the one who has lost your purpose for attending church. You, the one struggling to hold back the ocean of your past. You, the one who finds yourself continually backsliding. And you, the one who has lost your joy.

This book is written to the professional church player, I used to be you. If I were to be honest with myself, on occasion, I still struggle with being real in church and playing along with the crowd. I write to you as a recovered Broke Down Christian. As an individual who has been fully recovered in many ways, and now with an understanding of my own broken Christianity, I write not to fix yours. In contrast, I write to encourage you to look to the Elohim (God our creator) so that He might recreate you and give you a new passion and love for Jesus. I write to inspire intentional Godly living.

In obedience, I have written this book to the young and young-at-heart who struggle to understand full commitment to God in a world so saturated with self-service, sex, insensitivity, violence, and hatred. It is my profound prayer that this book brings you as much conviction and hope as it has brought me. While in repair, I have learned that God has not given up on me, and He loves me enough to give me more opportunities to respond to His love than I deserve, and that same love applies to you. As time continues to shift, we must develop an urgent sense of passion about being a beacon of Christ's light, and a channel of His love and miraculous healing power.

You are in my thoughts as I write, and at the end of my life when I must give account to Jesus, I would like to have embodied Psalm 40:9-10 NLT:

"I have told all your people about your justice.

I have not been afraid to speak out,

as You, O Lord, well know.

I have not kept the good news of Your justice hidden in my heart;

I have talked about Your faithfulness and saving power.

I have told everyone in the great assembly

of Your unfailing love and faithfulness."


Therefore, I will honor this call of God on my past and present, and write to you, my brother and my sister. I am going to admit to you right now, there is no sugar coated truth in this book, not when your eternity, purpose and hope are on the line. I want you to be led to freedom by the truth from the scriptures found in these pages, like I have been led to freedom. The style of this book is different – there is no sequence of events or overt connection of sections. It is composed of journal entries, poems, and messages of struggle and prayer. We all need to know that we are not alone as we wrestle with ourselves and life's curveballs. This book is not written to make you feel comfortable with your Broken Down Christianity, it is about recognizing hope and restoration, exhortation and encouragement in The Lord. This book is about awakening LOVE FOR JESUS CHRIST, and allowing ourselves to be matured by the circumstances that love helps us endure.

I write to myself first as a young woman whose Christian journey started out so on fire for God, I was fully convinced that I could walk through a wall if God told me to do it. However, I allowed that fire to be doused by burdensome situations that made run away from God and toward poor choices and negative influences. When I got saved at 13, I wanted nothing more than to help save the world and make Jesus proud. But as I stumbled my way through television, friends, boyfriends, college, and constant defeat, I stopped living to consistently demonstrate my love for Christ through obedience. I found myself giving into temptation and could feel the conviction of the Holy Spirit so heavily in my Spirit and body, yet I would still *touch, taste, and handle the unclean thing*, only to end up crying out for forgiveness afterward.

When I turned 19, the friends who knew me as a praying, praising, and serving advocate, could no longer see a genuine desire for Christ in me. I began compromising on my values, and losing sight of where I wanted to go. People like me, who have come to a place of compromise, walk a fine line between life and death all the while tarnishing our witness. The days we do try to live our lives for Jesus become worthless in the eyes of those to whom we are sent. People like us have lost our sense of urgency to live true to Christ and fulfil purpose as He did. We live casually and callously because we refuse to understand the brevity of life.

So what is a Broke Down Christian? A Broke Down Christian is one who continues to tarnish their witness by misrepresenting Christ, someone who loves conditionally, and gives offense control of their relationships. A Broken Down Christian is someone whose mirror is the world rather than the Word of God. It is someone who has lost the art of genuine prayer and worship; someone who wants to reclaim the passion they once had for Christ but is discouraged by their own past, too hurt and too oppressed to believe they can have the freedom Christ died to give.

When I completed this book, I sat in awe thinking, "GOD

TRUSTED ME TO DO SOMETHING...HA!" He trusted me, the young girl who could barely keep a pair of earrings? WHAT! I count it one of my life's greatest honors to be chosen to write to you. I am blessed with the amazing chance to do something for God. Beloved, all of my past mistakes and all that life has imposed on me have come full circle through the words on these pages. I GET TO tell you, Christian to Christian that you must examine yourself daily, that you need to put to death the deeds of the flesh (Rom 8:13) and put on the Lord Jesus Christ (Rom 13:14). I GET TO tell you to live like you were created to be loved and to let that unconditional love flow through you like the blood in your veins. Paul called himself the chief sinner, and could you imagine his own feelings that Jesus Himself commissioned him for a great work, a work that brought the gospel to the entire world? It is my great hope that you will overcome by the blood of Jesus Christ and the word of my testimony, so that your own testimony will awaken a responsive love for God in you, a love that is demonstrated outwardly and privately.

The question now is what in the world is this book supposed to contribute to your Christian walk, and why should you read it?

1. Confession: "Therefore confess your sins to each other and pray for each other so that you may be healed. The prayer of a righteous person is powerful and effective (James 5:16 NIV)." Confession is the first step to change, so acknowledging that you are a Broke Down Christian is key, if you need permission, take it from my confession.

2. Clarity: Recognizing that you are a sinner is one thing, but knowing what to do with that awareness is what leads to

transformation – the same concept applies to our broken down condition as Christians. After you have confessed your new found awareness about your condition, you would need clarity on three things: 1. What is broken? 2. How did you get that way? 3. How to recover?

3. Community: The Bible admonishes believers to confess their sins "one to another". Because community is essential, you need to know you are not alone in your journey and that you have support as you go through God's deliverance process. In this sobering self-examination, you have support as you run from compromise and forfeiture towards consistent passion, purpose and wholeness in Christ.

# A PRAYER FOR YOU

Our Father, who art in heaven, hallowed be Thy name, Thy kingdom, Thy will be done, on earth as it is in heaven.  I pray Lord that You would touch the hearts of everyone reading this book, break the stony hearts Father and make it flesh, that the scripture references would take root and not be stolen away by the enemy.  As they read Lord, speak to their very soul and call them out of darkness into your marvelous light.  I pray God that each reader submits to Your Holy Spirit permeating every area of their lives that they might be sanctified through and through.  Restore to them the joy of Your salvation, and to those who are on the verge of spiritual coma, Father, revive them by Your word.  Oh Lord, open their hearts, eyes and minds to see and experience Your intense, constant, and precise love.

Even so Father, I come against the spirit of misdirected offense, I pray that those reading would choose not to be offended, but to rebuke the devil and rejoice because You only correct those You love and care about.  Cause them to rejoice in the truth rather than sulk into a lie; show readers their own image in comparison with the image of them that You see when you look through time.  I thank You for breakthroughs, deliverance, healing, CHANGE, and the responsive, vigorous, and active love for Jesus being awakened in all of us.

In the mighty name of Jesus Christ our soon coming King I pray,

Amen.

LASHONDA JEAN-JACQUES

# 1
# BROKE DOWN SELF

I am my teenage parents' mistake,

I am the product of unsafe sex,

I am the seed of lust and yet more than any of these things...

I am God's imagination come to life.

I am certainly foolish,

And sometimes my choices are wise,

In between all of it I can be fearful,

But more than all of it I am evidence that God is ALIVE.

I have done stupid things with my body,

And at times let self-loathing consume my mind

And still somehow, the mind of Christ wants to be one with mine.

I've been selfish, I've been crazy,

I've thought myself worthless,

I have hated myself to the point of wanting death,

And yet The Christ came & died so life can flow inside of me.

You see, to my own amazement and everyone's confounding,

Living waters flow within me.

The Holy Spirit has found residence in my existence.

Jesus became all my broken pieces and when His body was broken they became whole.

Alone, I am a mess...

With Him, with Christ—I have been transformed.

I have become worthy. I have become worthy.

I have become worthy.

Goodness gracious —

I, LaShonda Jean-Jacques, have become worthy!

# SNAPSHOTS & SELFIES

I love a good selfie, it usually takes about 30 shots to find the perfect one and even then, I adjust the brightness, contrast, and maybe add a filter. All of this work is done to showcase the very best image. My Instagram (IG) displays fewer selfies than handwritten scriptures and prayers because that is who I am, but I recall a time when I needed to break away from social media because the selfies of those I followed became a stumbling block for me. Social media in general began to encourage jealousy, comparison, and ungratefulness in my heart. Although I would hit the "like" button on many pictures, I did so because I wanted what the picture portrayed. The more luxury I saw, the more I resented my humble lifestyle. Instead of setting goals that were true to myself, I began to covet and waste time daydreaming about having someone else's lifestyle. Furthermore, it drove me to try to create content that displayed a false reality of excess and indulgence. Through my selfies, I was motivated to pretend, envy, and covet. At the same time, I struggled to find gratitude for my own blessings. I knew then, just like I know now, that this mentality did not please God. But until I decided to fast away from social media, I was bound.

Conversations with others have taught me that I was not alone in my covetousness. After graduating college, a number of people I had the pleasure of catching up with experienced the same trappings of comparison and covetousness. Seeing the success of other college colleagues compared to their own caused them to diminish the significance of their journey and lose focus on where they were going, which made them feel less than their peers.

Comparison may show up uninvited but it doesn't stay when unwelcomed. When comparison enters your thoughts, its only intention is breaking you down and driving you towards a valley of discontentment. I call discontentment a valley because when you are in that deep, dark place, you rationalize that everyone around you is happier, successful, and living a more peaceful and abundant life than you are, while somehow doing it all with ease. What's worse, is that comparison causes you to idolize people and their lifestyles, which consequently makes them your god and you the servant.

Sometimes comparison drives you to compete with others to feed your pride, your pain, or an insatiable ego. You strive to be the best and out-do all those around you, not because it may benefit the future for you and your loved ones, but because your ego was hurt by rejection or the idea that you are being outdone. Beloved, you cannot compete with other people in life. Someone will always fall short and someone will always end up in the valley of discontentment. I know you may be thinking, "But what about healthy competition between friends? The Bible says that iron sharpens iron." I do not seek to dispute scripture, but to encourage you to not use it to justify wrong thinking; social media drives few people to healthy competition. Don't be driven to competition just to have nicer highlight reel of selfies than someone else.

Social media is a vehicle that can take you in either direction, right or wrong. It can drive you crazy or simply encourage you to be a better. Now, I love to follow Bible study pages, financial groups, and planning pages because every time I see a post, I am reminded of God's word or being disciplined. However, there was a time where I followed the pages of many "perfect-bodied" women, and in doing so, I welcomed comparison and opened my gates to discontentment. Soon, I was back in the mirror picking at my body and trying hard to visualize what I would look like with that woman's butt and this woman's hair. It became severely distracting to the point where I invested money into fad teas and started unhealthy eating habits. I even wore a waist cincher for 10 hours daily, because I was unhappy with myself again after spending years practicing gratitude for my body. I had become so discontent that I started complaining constantly to my husband about my body – the same body he loves and cherishes. Shaming my own body was something I practiced regularly, and although God had delivered me, I returned to that oppression from which I had been delivered.

We are like the Isrealites in the wilderness, even though God delivered them from the slavery of Egypt, they still found themselves longing for its slavery, as if the grass was greener there. Social media provides us with many opportunities to return to the oppressions from which we have been delivered. Snapshots and selfies on social media make Egypt look beautiful and bountiful even though we know we were slaves when we lived there. These idolized images make us want to belong and be admired. When I was a child, my elementary school had a dress-up day, and students paid $2 to be allowed to dress out of uniform for the day. On that day, I was so embarrassed that my mother sent me to school in straight leg jeans (when wide leg jeans was the trend), a black turtleneck (in SEPTEMBER in THE BAHAMAS), and some $5 wedges made of foam and straw. When I got to school, I was teased ruthlessly and remember running into the bathroom to cry. At break-time, I retreated to homeroom to avoid being seen by more students and teased even further. When my teacher asked me why I was crying, I told him about being teased because of how I was dressed. He then asked me a key question: "Why is it important if they like how you are dressed?" Through my tears, I replied "They are my friends and I want to fit in with them, I do not want to be an outsider."

We often focus so hard on comparing and competing that we struggle with the idea of being imperfect. We've been fooled into thinking that we have to be identical to our peers in order to belong. We are not okay with being odd and sometimes isolated. The desire to belong is natural, and so we determine our ability to belong by judging ourselves against the traits and possessions of those that seem to belong. Social media is a vehicle that helps us see even more of what more people have that we don't.

So here's where it got tough for me when examining my own heart during my fast away from social media: Why is it that we want to judge how acceptable we are against others, but when it comes to living for Christ, we cannot judge ourselves against God's word? We can figure out what it takes to belong to the in-crowd, and perform any manner of activities to appear worthy of acceptance by constantly filtering and editing ourselves until we are acknowledged. However, because a true relationship with Christ requires so much more, including self-denial, we run from the challenge of discipline and love. We want to be able to take selfies of ourselves to look like we belong with all the perfect people on social media, but we are not able to truly belong to Christ because our snapshots, selfies, and filters don't look like Christ, let alone resemble Him. Let's be honest, in order to appear more 'Christian' than we truly are, we post a daily scripture or share a sermonette, so we can belong with the social media Christians. As humans, our social media serves to influence where we put our cash and how we spend our time. But as Christians, social media should be a tool for us to influence on Christ's behalf and be spurred on to good works. The people we choose to follow effect how we are influenced, not because they have power over us, but because we don't have power over ourselves.

I am writing to myself first, because the truth is, I've spent more time on Instagram gazing at selfies, than I have gazing at Jesus and laying down my life every day to get this book out before now! Because of my own weaknesses, I've spent more time trying to look like the world with a little Jesus in me, than I have trying to be Jesus' selfie to the world. If we are supposed to be representing Jesus here on earth through service, love, prayer, forgiveness, and by sharing the gospel, then shouldn't we be striving and working to be just that? How can we have energy to work for Jesus and be truly changed by His word if we are drained from comparing ourselves with other selfies and constantly being stuck in the valley of discontentment?

It is truly time to take charge of your happiness and your inner peace. If you have time to scour Instagram (IG), you have time to invest into working toward a passion that feeds your heart. Time to peruse IG means you have time to figure out how long it will take you to save money you earned legally without compromising your values, to buy that house or go on that vacation. Time for IG means you have time to curate authentic life experiences that will inspire others as you have been inspired.

Then there are those of us – the observers – who get sucked in and begin to envy the false approval that comes with all the likes, shares, and comments on social media. The Word of God blew my mind with James 3:13-16, which says that where envy and self-seeking are, confusion and every evil thing are also. When we do things out of envy and with a self-serving motive, God has no part in it and every evil thing is present. It seems off the wall, but the King James Version, New King James Version, and the New Living Translation of the Bible says, "every evil thing/work" is there. Meanwhile, our heavenly Father has the displeasure of watching us submit ourselves to the slavery of envy, covetousness, pride, comparison, and ungratefulness as we quest for perfect snapshots and selfies that exclude Him. He is grieved that we are so discontent and unable to see the true treasure of life that is before us – a relationship with Him through Jesus Christ. He does not want us to become lost in the unreal, forgetting that:

1. There is a war going on for our attention and we can't focus on strategy and execution if we are distracted! We spend more time using social media to look for motivation, #goals, likes,

outfits, hairstyles, and reasons to degrade ourselves, than we do looking for ourselves in Him. We are distracted! We do not go away with Him anymore on intimate spiritual journeys of prayer, fasting, and fellowship. Even now, I am reminded of Hosea and his prostitute wife. Similar to his wife, God's chosen people have not stopped prostituting to the world. We have become weak, because The Word is not in us to the degree that it should be. As a result we not only struggle to live the Word but to receive it from others, then find ourselves retreating to offense rather than rising up to maturity. Distraction has caused our passion for Christ to wane. We pursue things and people outside of His will because we no longer actually know what His will is. IT'S TIME TO WAKE UP!

2. Being driven to discontentment means we have looked past Him and His love, and instead look to the world for fulfillment. If we really believe in 1 Timothy 6:6, which says, "true contentment coupled with godliness is great gain," then we would be seeking God wholeheartedly for this "true contentment" of which Apostle Paul speaks.

3. What you feed lives, but what you nourish thrives. At some point, we must decide to come away with God, and designate time for Him daily where there are no distractions. My husband and I became parents in June of 2016, and I realized that finding time to do anything with a newborn baby is quite difficult. Rather than use my son as an excuse not to dedicate time to Him, I included him in my daily devotions. I have witnessed my aunt, a mother of three children, maintain a full-time job, attend university, and remain active in ministry, all while rising at 5:00AM every morning without fail to seek God. Rather than taking 10 minutes in the morning to scroll

through IG, choose those 10 minutes to pray, to write to Him, or to read God's written word.

Beloved, we have to nurse the passion for Jesus Christ within us. We have to feed our desires for a better standard of living by running to the One who died for us to experience abundant life. Jesus' death has given us believers access to abundant joy, peace, contentment, and this strange ability to cheer others on, even in our own successes or failures. We must nourish our desires to be a selfie of Jesus here on earth with service and discipline, so that when envy and comparison knock on the door of our hearts and minds, we let it be known that they are not welcomed and submit them to Christ.

4. Social media has a time and place, and that place is NOT meant to dictate our choices and attitudes. What occurs on social media should not possess enough power to cause any of us to change our course to seek "Instafame" rather than seeking God. A question in my spirit that I often hear is, "How can a man submit to technology (your own creation), but can't submit to God, your Creator?" We've been deceived – we recognize God as Creator but have been imprinted upon by another master that we consult for everything. When you can't help but tell social media every detail of your life and use it to vent every personal frustration, you have resorted to consulting it. When you find yourself stalking the pages of others you claim not to like, you feed envy. When you find yourself obsessively checking how many likes your selfie received and feeling proud that people liked a picture of you, it is reflective of your need for validation from social media.

I imagine our Creator thinking about how humanity has become so degraded. Man is not at the pinnacle of evolution but we have regressed to a lesser form. We have access to more information about everything we could imagine, including Jesus, yet we are not smarter. In fact, we are more ignorant than ever. We cannot separate the lie from the truth; reality and social media's filtered pictures have merged into one. This reminds me of Jeremiah 18:1-4, which describes how the potter smashed the clay and began again because it did not turn out the way he wanted. I am thankful that God's mercy is everlasting, but I am also thankful that He loves us enough to crush us in ways that will not kill us, but to re-shape us instead.

This book is my new beginning! It is my cross to bear for this era of life, it is my practice in discipline and service, and it is the fruit of obedience despite procrastination. When I graduated college, I was fully decided that I was going to graduate school; I even had a scholarship to a prestigious institution. In the summer of 2013, God crushed my plans and my image of who I thought I was and was meant to be. Obtaining my college degree was a major deal for me because it was a next level achievement, as my parents barely made it through high school. My mother's dream came true; my father was so proud. Yet, there I was, stuck on my grandmother's bathroom floor in Opa Locka, Florida searching for God and my life. I remember distinctly weeping, upset that I wasn't going to grad school that Fall. I remember even more when The Holy Spirit spoke to me and asked, "How can you esteem a degree over time spent with Me?" My answer remained the same from elementary school, only taking on a more elaborated form, "I want to have something to show that my peers and family would deem worthy of rejoicing and bragging. They would understand me through academic achievement better than they would through pursuing You Lord." I was looking to be accepted, I was looking for more to compete with, I was looking for things to post on social media that would gather likes and cheerleading. When I sit amongst my peers, I wanted to have something that was impressive to share by their standards. Academia was a filter on my selfies and snapshots that I could hide behind. I wanted people to be able to say, "Boy Shonda always been smart," just as they repeatedly said when I was growing up.

For a year I drifted between my quiet place on the bathroom floor and on my grandmother's couch as I dove into The Word – worshiping, truly seeking God, and looking for my place in this world. Over time, it finally hit me that I do not have a place in this world, but rather I operate in this world for a place in eternity. Not that I could ever earn eternity, for it is a gift, but I must act in obedience so as not to forfeit such a priceless and indescribable gift. Whenever people experience my behavior and attitudes they receive a snapshot of me, and because I call myself a Christian they associate that snapshot with Christ. If those experiences are filled with pride, judgement, arguments, poor attitude, and indiscipline, then those same people will associate these negative attributes with their understanding of Christianity. When I assess myself through the Word of God, I want to be assured that I represented Christ well.

# SHAME

When I think about shame, I think about Adam and Eve, and how they hid from God after sinning. When God asked them their reason for hiding, they admitted to their shame for being naked (Gen 3:10). Take a moment to examine the cunning of the serpent – not only did he convince Eve to eat that fruit which she in turn fed to her husband, he somehow unlocked something in her that made her ashamed of how she was created. God made Adam and Eve naked, but sin made them put on clothing and feel shame for their nakedness. Do you see where I am going? The devil will come to sneakily take away your peace about how God made you and remade you.

In the case of the repented individual, the enemy schemes to make you ashamed of what you have done, so that even though God has forgiven your sins and made you a new creation, you feel the need to hide and cover yourself with shame. God made you naked! When I say naked, I do not mean physically naked, I mean emotionally and spiritually naked with Him, willingly exposed and fully showing all of who you are to Him as though it were natural to you. God created you to be vulnerable to His love. So when the enemy comes against you and your repented heart trying to entice you to give way to the spirit of shame, keep 1 John 3:20 in mind and rebuke him, for God is greater than those feelings of guilt.

Beloved, God did not give you the spirit of fear and He surely did not equip His children with the spirit of shame, therefore, you do not have time to be ashamed about your past. Being ashamed of your past causes you to hoard it, when in reality God wants to free you of shame and guilt so that the very past that separated you from Him will become the platform upon which you present Him to others. God will not waste any of your past or your pain, He will deliver and heal you of it. There is evidence of His promise to us in the Bible. Romans 10:11 says, "God will not allow believers to be put to shame." Similarly, Isaiah 50:7 states that "Because God is our helper we have not been disgraced." You have got to dig into the Bible to fortify your mind and fight off the enemy's enticements to condemn yourself and doubt God's power to forgive and love you. Shame has the power to creep in and make you perceive God's love as conditional. It is important for me to highlight for you that I am not talking about a shame that drives you to repentance for a sin you committed. For example, the shame Peter felt after denying Jesus three times was appropriate and it led to repentance and carrying out the assignment Jesus gave him to strengthen his brothers (Luke 22:32). The spirit of shame discussed here specifically references a stifling of growth and the encouragement of isolation from Christ.

Even when I was passionately active in my Christian faith as a teenager, somehow I began to question the reality of my salvation; could God really save me? Are my sins really forgiven and forgotten (Heb 8:12)? Have all my sins been blotted away (Is 43:25)? Every time I saw a piece of my past, I would shudder in shame, even though there is no shame for forgiven sins.

Let me testify. Growing up in the Bahamas, it was a shameful thing to have HIV/AIDS, Well, my mother died of AIDS-related illness when I was 13 years old, and I was ashamed. When asked how my mother died, I would tell a half-truth by saying she had kidney problems (she had the problems because of AIDS). Because of my shame, I could not bring myself tell anyone that my beautiful mother with her gorgeous figure, had "the whammy" as it was called. It was not until I was 16 that my Spanish teacher and father asked me how my mom passed and I said "it was a total body shut down." In Spanish, he replied "SIDA (AIDS)?" I remember the long pause before I spoke the truth for the first time. That moment changed my life for the better. You see, although I had nothing to do with my mother's cause of death, her sins of fornication bound me to shame and made me a liar. When we let go of the lies and the past we are holding onto, we do not have to be ashamed. No one can make us feel ashamed because our Father offers us liberty from that shame, we just need to be honest about it.

Shame is debilitating and it hinders us from tasting and seeing the goodness of God. It hampers our ability to effectively engage with our kingdom assignments, and an ineffective

Christian is a Broke Down One. Philippians 3:13-14 AMP (Amplified Bible) says, "Brothers and sisters, I do not consider that I have made it my own yet; but one thing I do: forgetting what lies behind and reaching forward to what lies ahead, I press on toward the goal to win the [heavenly] prize of the upward call of God in Christ Jesus." When we repent and our sins are forgiven, we then have to focus on what lies ahead and winning the heavenly prize. Throughout the books that Apostle Paul wrote, he acknowledged that he was a chief sinner to edify and encourage other believers, not to revisit the past and beat himself up. Could you imagine if after meeting Jesus on the road to Damascus, Paul decided he would shudder in shame and shrink away from the purpose of Christ for his life? What would have happened to the Gentiles?

Let me testify once again. After fornicating, there was such a godly sorrow in my life, that I repented and accepted God's forgiveness, or so I thought. Unfortunately, I soon acquainted myself with an ungodly shame when the hurt of past molestations and the shame of poor choices began to plague my thoughts. This type shame is ungodly because it didn't go away, and no matter how much I apologized to God, it was still there. I was being held hostage and I did not run to God with this new found shame, so not only did I put on fig leaves and hide from God like my parents Adam and Eve, I hid from the truth and constructive criticism of other believers. Further, that shame resulted in me running back to its roots instead of running to God and letting Him uproot it and my guilt. So, because I couldn't accept God's forgiveness and continually beat myself up about my choice, my poor choice was all I could focus on. I was single minded about the wrong thing and struggled to overcome my thoughts. Consequently, these thoughts prevented me from helping others believe that God truly forgives and loves unconditionally.

Beloved, shame not only affects us spiritually, it also impacts our daily lives. Shame caused me to run from God and right back into the same sin. In doing so, I put myself at risk for many things, including STDs, unwanted pregnancy, an abortion, and single motherhood. Shame binds us up so tight that it makes us commit a slow and torturous suicide if we don't find freedom. Don't believe me? Ask my mother why she never got treatment until it was too late, or ask her why she never told her family members she was HIV-positive in order to get support. Shame shaped her choices and disabled her from making the right ones, just like it did for me.

I can imagine the look on our Father's face when His children surrender to shame instead of surrendering to His love. I can imagine hearing His thoughts saying, "No My child, don't hide it away, bring it to Me, I am not bruised by your hurt. I understand you and I love you. Let me love you out of shame and regret into freedom, peace, and rejoicing." I know I am doing a lot of imagining but Beloved, I truly can imagine God thinking those words when you sit and wallow in shame because of your past. Surrender your shame to God. He is listening, He is so loving, and I am truly amazed at the power of His love to heal a Christian broken down by shame. When ungodly shame is released, it gives you power to unveil yourself so that you can be a more effective Christian. It gives you the strength to reveal your testimony, which will help someone else do the same. By surrendering your shame, you become the very proof that God delivers us from self-constructed strongholds. Just surrender.

# CHAMBER OF SECRETS

"What happens in this house, stays in this house." This phrase was something I heard all too often growing up, and I never understood why it was so important to my mother and others that I keep the tragedies of home to myself. Why was anyone requiring me as a child, to bear an unbearable burden? I learned early on that secrets are killers; they are joy killers, peace stealers, and family disrupters.

Let me break it down like this:

In the darkness of the many apartments that I lived in as a young child, there was molestation, spousal rape, self-neglect, and violence of all kinds. In spite of the seriousness of these tragedies, speaking of these issues was not an option because they all fell under the same rule: "What happens in this house stays in this house." I am certain that my mother intended no harm when she passed this rule down to me. After all, people only repeat what they know to do. But it is also clear that she didn't have the wisdom to know that living in darkness for fear of public humiliation is poisonous. When my mother died, I realized that I was no longer trapped within the walls and limitations of "the house". Instead, I decided that I needed to place myself under God's protection, which meant exposing the hidden secrets to His purifying and guilt-free light.

Before I'd even turned 10 years old, I'd become a victim of molestation at the hands of a close family member. Although there were a few people who knew, they chose not to expose the secret to anyone who could help. In their minds, my issue "wasn't their problem" and it was more important to them to protect the clean image of the house. When I was molested again, this time by a close friend of my mother, I submitted to the norms of my surroundings and remained silent. As a child, I came to the understanding that molestation was an unspoken norm of the life I knew. There was no protection, and any attempts to speak out would lead to people talking badly about my mother and family.

When my step-father became my molester, I finally broke my silence. After telling my mother my secret, I was ripped from my home and sent to live with family. Instead of punishment, my offender got to stay in the house to maintain the image of a healthy family life. When my mom finally passed away, a cousin let it slip that her parents knew what was happening to me, but never spoke up. In that moment, I felt confused, hurt, and alone. The same burning questions repeatedly consumed my thoughts: "Why didn't anyone protect me? Why didn't anyone help me?" All those years, I was protecting the home at the expense of my innocence and understanding of love. When I finally decided to use my voice to protect myself, I was abandoned.

Do you see what I am saying beloved? When you protect the house the first time, you can easily slip into a dangerous cycle of abuse. Sometimes, you cannot depend on your mother or others that you love, because they too were abused yet survived – and expect you to do the same. And often, that cycle is passed down through generations. It is likely that your grandmother faced the same type of abuse and raised your mother to mask her pain with the same silence that she taught you. Protecting the house either starts or continues dangerous generational patterns that will cripple and kill if not exposed. The impulse to protect the house can be suffocating, similar to weeds in a garden. Like weeds strangling blossoming plants, your conformity to abuse hinders the growth of the seeds of God's love planted inside of you. It may cause you to think, "God, I know You see what's going on with me, why aren't You doing anything?" As these feelings and questions build, you begin to resent your relationship with God.

Beloved, sexual assault should never be protected. Keeping these secrets hidden protects the criminal and puts others at risk, while simultaneously binding the victim to the past. I learned to protect the house is too protect the work of the enemy and giving him a safe playground to try and destroy futures. YOU HAVE GOT TO EXPOSE THE HOUSE, EXPOSE THAT WORK OF THE DEVIL! Sometimes, it may be too late to call the police for help, but it is never too late to get counseling and allow God to take the lead on your road to recovery. The sick part about protecting the house is that the poisonous wrongdoer is protected at the expense of others. While I was being secretly molested, my relationship with my mother suffered, she remained bound in an unhealthy marriage, and my siblings were at risk of the same dangers I experienced. In the midst of it all, my stepfather was free to roam in and out of bedrooms at night.

God does not desire for us to be slaves to our disabling secrets. Furthermore, He does not desire for us to be liars, claiming to be free but still wearing shackles. He wants us to live in the light and walk in truth. Before being delivered from the shackles of abuse and the residue it left on my heart and mind, I refused to tell anyone that I was a victim of molestation, especially at the hands of a family member. I spent so much time protecting the house that I did not see that it made me hateful, unforgiving, bitter, and untrusting toward men. Anytime I was alone with a man or embraced by one, my only perception was that he wanted to make the encounter sexual. My mind was immediately drawn to the most perverse actions that may have gone through his mind. If I allowed my mind to linger for too long, I could visualize myself being abused by that person and would immediately feel hatred begin to boil up inside of me. I don't remember how or why, but I finally spoke up and confessed to some girlfriends that I was molested, only to find out that some of them were also victims.

If you decide to protect the house, for fear of shame, separation, loss of relationship or whatever reason, you will do it again, and again, and then you will require it of your child. No matter your situation, I encourage you not to protect the house. Stop protecting poisonous secrets that make you feel forsaken by God, dirty, and worthless. Please seek help! You are worth whatever it takes to help you heal. Take it before Jesus beloved, and let Him show you the light. Let Him relieve you of your burden and replace your sorrows with joy.

For many years, I was paranoid; I felt worthless, used, and dirty. Each day I bathed in those dirty secrets, not knowing that I could be freed. Thankfully, I now have truth, a peaceful truth that flows over me like fresh water. I have gained freedom from the secrets that were locked away in that protected house, and now I have a testimony of overcoming and experiencing God's love where the pain of life was most intense. Abuse is so common in our communities and we are so busy protecting our houses that we don't understand that the freedom is in the telling, the healing is in the sharing, and the protecting comes in knowing you are not alone and that there are others who will act on your behalf.

Beloved, do not sacrifice yourself to protect the house. If you are experiencing abuse of any kind, seek help and seek a way out. If there is someone you trust, tell them you need them. Move beyond the prejudices that often revolve around therapy and look to a professional therapist to help you unload your thoughts. Abuse is traumatic. Even though it may be a memory from your past, it can wield a powerful grip on all future relationships. Can you imagine having a child and not wanting to leave them alone with your spouse because your mother's husband molested you and that poisonous secret has begun to poison your view of your husband? Can you imagine being intimate with your spouse and having flash backs of your abuser during a moment of God-ordained passion and oneness? I've been there, and too many times my flashbacks caused me to mentally check out during our intimate time. When I think about the stronghold that my past held on me, I have to pause and praise God for His deliverance.

God does not desire that your past strangle your future. Lessons and deliverance from the past help to motivate His beloved children toward a future that embraces the freedom of His love and salvation. I know He has a place for this pain in your future, I know from experience that God Himself will turn your valley of trouble into a gateway of hope (Hosea 2:15). It is not God's will that you are violated, or a recipient of fraudulent love. However, it is His will that you surrender the chaos of your pain in exchange for His peace. It is God's will that you are not bound like a slave to those life experiences that put you on the brink of emotional or physical death.

He desires that you live an abundant life as His new creation in Christ. Beloved, freedom is in God's plans for you.

# A PRAYER FOR YOU

Dear Lord Jesus,

We struggle with so many things as believers, especially the shame we feel over any poor decisions we've made once becoming Christians. We know Lord that godly shame is meant to drive us to repentance and not away from You, and we ask that You help us identify the shame in our lives that puts distance between us and Your will. This shame makes us think we are unworthy of love, even though Your very sacrifice on Calvary declares us worthy. Deliver us oh Lord, not only from shame, but the lies we tell our fellow brothers and sisters when they ask about our honest well-being. Drive us to overcome this fear of transparency and intimacy with you Lord. Remove the fig leaves of shame that place a barrier between us and the cleansing truth of the Word of God. Give us the wisdom and courage to pour out the pain of the past, the pain our mothers and aunts required us to bury when they told us to keep deadly secrets. Purge us, keep us from contaminating our future vision with those of the past, and protect us from endangering our present.

We want to be effective for Your glory, we want to have a testimony to help others regain intimacy with You. You bore all of our shame on Calvary Jesus, so that we did not have to carry the burden. We are called to "put on the Lord Jesus Christ," but how can we be selfies of You when we are bound to shame, comparison, competition and jealousy? Deliver us oh Lord so that our love for You, ourselves, and our neighbors will flourish and reproduce fruit after its own kind.

Amen.

# UNWORTHY

Before my son was born, I expected a visit from a house guest who is accustomed to the finer things in life, and although we have a wonderful relationship, I felt intimidated by her impending arrival. I told myself "I need a new pot set," and "This sunken couch just won't do, she's going to be disgusted." I rambled on for quite some time in my head about all the things that were not perfect for someone of her caliber. I even imagined us no longer being friends after she left because she would surely have an opinion I didn't like about the quality of my cookware and furniture. In hindsight, my anxieties all seem quite silly. Without proof, I decided for myself that my friend would interrupt the peace of my home with negative words and attitudes about my possessions.

Even though I am very content with my home and proud of the furniture that I do have, I decided that my home was not good enough for her to visit and that the true condition of my life was unworthy of her presence. Doubtfulness is a horrible habit that I've struggled with for quite some time. I count myself out based on others' resumes, what others have or are accustomed to, and as a result become ungrateful for my own blessings. My couch with its sunken center is a blessing from God. It is the product of the financial discipline that my husband and I used to save for the furnishings in our home. That couch represents our decision to put away foolish financial behavior and mature. That in itself is a reason to celebrate.

Beloved, too many of you are in this same boat with me. I know that dirt is never unique; there is always someone who has played in the same dirt you have. After being honest with God in prayer about how I was feeling, I realized that I don't get to feel unworthy because of what someone else has. Why? Because it makes me ungrateful, a complainer, and causes me pull away from good people because of concocted scenarios in my head. You see, even if a person is disgusted by the humility of your lifestyle, THAT IS NOT YOUR BUSINESS!!! Just as I advise that you shouldn't take it personal when someone else is succeeding faster than you are, you shouldn't take someone having more expensive possessions personal either. There is no need to try to "keep up with the Joneses". Doing so is not pleasing unto God, and He does not want us running back to the pits of envy and ungratefulness.

For example, maybe you had a credit score of 450 three years ago, but now it is 600 and you can afford more than you ever have. Look at your growth!!! Celebrate your growth!! You're not growing to compete with your neighbor; your growth should focus on where you are now in comparison to where God is calling you to be. Just because you can't pray for two hours weeping before the Lord like Sister Mary, does not make you unworthy to lead prayer. You may not have a revelatory grasp on the scriptures like a minister, but that should not stop you from sharing how those scriptures have touched your heart and changed your life!

You are not unworthy of people who are different from you. Do not get sucked in by the enemy's scheme to dim your light by making you believe that your peers are your competition, rather than individuals with whom you can celebrate and share wisdom. My dear friend would probably laugh in my face if she heard the conversation I had in my head about how I imagined she would treat me. And what's worse, she would likely be offended that I would think such low thoughts of her! I pray that we all keep in mind that Christ died for us to live abundantly. And while your abundance may look different from mine, my own abundance will not be diminished by our differences.

# 2

# BROKE DOWN NEIGHBORING

Sometimes in life we get thirsty, we become so parched—dehydrated even. We find ourselves empty and listless, maybe hallucinating from abject thirst. Then someone comes along and you learn that their name is water and shelter. They may not have all the resources to pull you out of the blazing sun, but they care enough to cover you with their own coat, tent, or back. They see how cracked your lips are and recognize your need for water, and they offer you revival. They are unafraid to put their lips on yours and fill your lungs with oxygen. They are unafraid to take their own canteen and wet your face, and quench your current thirst. To all the people who have been water in my life, this is for you. To all the people that struggle to be water passing by parched people, this is for you. For all the people that need water, this is for you.

--LaShonda Jean-Jacques

# LOVE MY NEIGHBOR LIKE MYSELF?

Mark 12:31 AMP "This is the second: 'You shall [unselfishly] love your neighbor as yourself.' There is no other commandment greater than these."

Romans 15:2 AMP "Let each one of us [make it a practice to] please his neighbor for his good, to build him up spiritually."

How we treat people is a reflection of how we truly believe we deserve to be treated. Furthermore, how we treat others is a reflection of how we treat Jesus. It's no wonder that we can't spend time in God's word or in prayer faithfully, because we are just as fickle in our human relationships. At times, we may express dislike for certain people, but it is likely that those feelings stem from having a serious problem within ourselves and with Jesus. Personally, I still struggle so deeply with liking people. And quite frankly, sometimes I don't even like myself. My apprehension towards some people makes it hard to them reach for Jesus. I was filthy, I was dead in the grave, and yet God still looked through the eons of time and decided He wanted intimate fellowship with me. *Me*, of all people. So I find myself wondering yet again, if God looked through the glass of time and decided to associate in the greatest and most intimate way possible with me, who am I to treat others like Christ didn't also die for them?

Beloved, our way of neighboring has deviated from God's plan, especially when we can no longer confess our sins one to another. When a believer cannot come to you to find correction, compassion, prayer, and confidentiality, we have lost a major part of the art of neighboring. We live in a time where we have become numbed to our surroundings, and the boundaries of our active concern are limited to our family and friends. Beloved family, this way of thinking is dangerous. We were never created to isolate ourselves from loving others. Believers are purposed to stimulate and reproduce the unconditional and extravagant love of God as we journey through life.

# DON'T WATCH ME DIE

We live in a world where people will pull their phones out to record tragedy and injustice for the sake of entertainment, but won't get involved to help. In a similar way, we sit by and watch family, friends, strangers, and associates die spiritually. We see people's hopes being crushed, and yet we do not act. As those in need struggle to cope, they forget that God is mindful of them and help is on the way (YOU). They are weighed down by depression, bills, medical problems, and loneliness. Those of us who can help bear their burdens may offer to "keep them in prayer", but do nothing more. Sometimes doing more is as simple as giving a hot meal to a homeless person or helping a struggling parent by helping to pay for their groceries. We see people broken down in all kinds of ways and yet we refuse to let our "light so shine before men that they would see and glorify our Father which is in heaven", as stated in Matt 5:16. We hide the Christianity we have, forgetting that Jesus would have had compassion on those in need. He would have fed them and alleviated their burdens, especially the spiritual ones. Jesus would have let His light shine so that they could see God in Him. Are we showing people how God lives in us?

Too many of us are displaying a conditional love of Christ, when the true form of Christ's love has no condition. We must not allow our hearts to be hardened to the point that we are not touched by spiritual sickness and spiritual death. What if we began feeding the spiritually hungry, and allowed the light of Christ in us to shine everywhere we went? What if we started giving to those poor in money or encouragement? What if we began to intercede daily or weekly for those trying to overcome a particular lifestyle (sometimes I get a strong urge to pray for prostitutes and their children)? What if we began to act like Jesus, showing others His grace through our sensitivity, compassion, and care? What if we offered an encouraging word to the people who always seem depressed or upset? What if we helped someone see that they have something for which to be grateful? So many people are in the spiritual intensive care unit – they have been broken in ways we sometimes cannot imagine. They are experiencing levels of bondage to poverty, pain, and suffering that are beyond us. On the contrary, there are many of us who have been exceedingly blessed. We have our prayers that "availeth much", our bank accounts, vehicles, our clothes and shoes, our pantry and toiletries. We have all of these material things. But more importantly, we have our time and ears— to be a blessing to others, and to point them to Jesus. If we do it for them, we do it for Jesus (Mathew 25:35-40)!

"What good is it, my brothers, if someone says he has faith but does not have works? Can that faith save him? If a brother or sister is poorly clothed and lacking in daily food, and one of you says to them, "Go in peace, be warmed and filled," without giving them the things needed for the body, what good is that? So also faith by itself, if it does not have works, is dead. (James 2:14-17 (ESV)) "

The challenge facing the 21$^{st}$ century Christian is the temptation to listen to people's problems and respond with, "I'll pray for you." There is nothing wrong with praying for someone, for we know that we ought to pray without ceasing (1 Thes 5:16) and that God indeed responds to prayer. However, our faith is suffocated to death when we refuse to act. James 2:14-17 makes it very plain for believers, and expresses that you cannot just pray for people or wish them well when they have needs you can meet, especially if meeting their need does not prevent you from satisfying the needs of your own household. I pray God breaks our stony hearts and instills more desire in us to give freely. Although helping others leaves more opportunity to be deceived by people's falsified sob stories, we must understand that repeatedly being deceived means we need more discernment. It does not mean that we should refuse to help others beyond giving them a few lines during our prayer time.

Jesus is such a loving Jesus that He offers life to those who are dying. We have life inside of us, we have living water that will never dry up (John 7:38), and we can replenish people by the power of The Holy Spirit. There is someone out there who is severely dehydrated, and others who are thirsty and tired of fighting for their lives. We have the Source within us and He wants to operate through our actions. So I charge us, let us not sit idly by and watch anyone suffer, dial 911 (literally or in prayer) while you perform CPR (provide a need, encourage, empower, listen, be gentle, forgive, express honesty, and give love). Be led by The Spirit in all things, but for God's glory HELP!

We can even watch people die while sharing the gospel of Jesus Christ. When my mother was alive, I recall a three-month stretch of my childhood during which we did not have running water and had to get water from the pump every few days for hygiene and cooking. Many Christian people of different denominations came to share the gospel with us on the weekends. They left booklets to read but nothing more. Those that were aware of our struggle did not help us carry water from the pumps, or ask if we had lunch for school or funds for the laundromat. None of them asked my mother if she needed help establishing a budget so she could make sure the essential bills were always paid. But what they did offer were those booklets describing how Jesus loves us and "will provide all of our needs according to His riches in glory."

As an adult reflecting on that situation, I questioned their intentions. Did they expect us to see the Jesus they so passionately talked about while we were dragging five gallon jugs of pump water, or while we were eating cheap, salty noodles and Kraft dinners for every meal? Beloved, we cannot expect people to see Jesus in the dark of their homes, with no running water, and no sense of hope. The help we give them may or may not change their lives right away, but in those tough moments, we can always offer hope and support in the name of Jesus. For some people, you and I may be the only access to tasting and seeing the goodness of God.

I urge you to let the Holy Spirit invade your interactions with others so that you can demonstrate Christ by not only offering a gospel tract or pamphlet but also emotional, mental, or financial relief. Beloved, this is not a call for you to start handing out cash to every one you want to share the gospel with, this is a charge for you to remember that you have endless opportunities to do good works for others to see and glorify God (Mat 5:16). Whether your good work is sending a scripture or encouraging text a few times a week, helping a single mother purchase school supplies, or treating an overworked acquaintance to a lunch break, take it upon yourself to do the work. Sharing the gospel can be scary, especially since many people are serving "the universe," aligning their chakras or exploring other religions, but it must be done. Fellowshipping with other believers and interceding for them is another way to meet a deep spiritual need for those who are enduring hardship. Pray that you would receive the boldness it takes to share and demonstrate the gospel of Jesus Christ. Invite someone home for lunch after church, help serve in a soup kitchen, clear out your closet and give to someone who can use the clothing instead, pray for people when you say you will, carry hygiene packs in your car to give to the homeless – the opportunities to be of service are endless. There are so many ways we can represent God on earth, so many ways we can meet the physical needs of someone as a way to introduce them to Christ. In addition to sharing the gospel, pray and ask God to lead you.

Galatians 6:9 ESV (English Standard Version) "And let us not grow weary of doing good, for in due season we will reap, if we do not give up. "

Ephesians 2:10 (ESV) "For we are his workmanship, created in Christ Jesus for good works, which God prepared beforehand, that we should walk in them. "

# DO UNTO OTHERS...BECAUSE IT'S UNTO CHRIST

*"If you do it to the least of them, you do it into Me."* (Matt 25:45)

If we gossip about our neighbors, we have gossiped about Christ. When we have a bad attitude with them and refuse to interact with them, we refuse Christ. When we watch them suffer and don't offer help, we have done the same to Christ. When we do things to make others envy us, we do it to Jesus. When we are drawn to do these negative actions, we should ask ourselves, "Would I watch Jesus suffer? Would I share Jesus' confidential business that I know would make Him feel betrayed and hurt? Would I be jealous of Jesus? Would I try to make Jesus jealous of me?"

What would happen if we could just see Jesus in all of our neighbors? Yes, even the cursing, smoking, partying neighbor who disrespects your right to a good night's sleep. What if you could look at your neighbor and see Jesus on Calvary paying the ultimate price for their bad habits? You see beloved, that's the thing we have to grasp in order to love our neighbors more...Jesus already paid for the very thing that makes you struggle to be neighborly toward them. He paid for their nasty attitude, He paid for their violent words, He paid for their gossiping and sense of entitlement just like He paid for yours.

Everyone is a soul that Christ died for – even the racists, the abusers, the promiscuous, and both you and me. As a child, if I ever spoke about someone in a demeaning way, my aunt would always tell me, "Das a soul what Christ died for." Her message has stuck with me into adulthood. You don't get to charge people for their faults, because Jesus already paid for their sin with His life. However, what you get to do is be so unconditionally honest, gentle, respectful, compassionate, and humble that they recognize the power of Christ's love in you.

Beloved, your enemy is also your neighbor and as such, he must be loved, forgiven, and extended the same compassion that you would give to the people you hold close to your heart. The Bible tells us to clothe and feed even our enemies (Rom 12:20). Even as your enemy, what if your presence is the only example of Christ's love that person will ever know? By not loving your neighbor as yourself, you taint their understanding of Christ's love and place them in jeopardy of rejecting Christ. It is more important that your enemy responds to Christ's love than it is for you to be comfortable with how they choose to live their life. Only Christ has the power to change hearts and destructive lifestyles. Having a desire to see others redeemed means you have a desire to see the message of Christ thriving in this world. Do unto others as you'd want others to do unto you, because you are also doing so unto Christ.

# A PRAYER FOR US

Lord, please forgive us for delaying to pray and fast for someone, delaying to give, and worst of all, delaying to share the gospel. Please forgive our selfishness, we know that You desire that none perish. We call ourselves Your children, yet we sit by and watch people perish without speaking up. Father, please forgive us for giving into fear over someone's reputation. Forgive us for holding people's past against them, forgive us for misrepresenting Jesus. We thank You because You make all things new, including us. You qualify the disqualified and under qualified, and we thank You for it all. Keep us from deliberate sins that may cost us precious time.

In Jesus' name, I pray.

Amen.

# SELF LOVE = LOVING OTHERS

Ephesians 5:29 *"For no one ever hated his own flesh, but nourishes and cherishes it, just as Christ does the church..."*

The first major takeaway from this scripture is the idea that no one hates themselves, but we all nourish ourselves. Now we may not always nourish properly, but we all desire to nourish. The word nourish (Strong's 1625) means "to bring to maturity", which shows us that we love ourselves by ensuring we are growing and appreciating our own bodies. In order to love my neighbor like myself, I must not be hateful towards toward others. Instead, I must nurture them and contribute to their growth. To make the nourishment of ourselves and others a constant habit, we have to be willing to ask ourselves some important questions:

Are the interactions we have with others fruitful? Are people's lives better for having intertwined with ours? When engaging with a coworker, do our words, actions, and attitudes help mature that individual or do we stunt growth by feeding into gossip, over-indulging during happy hour, or showing up late to work without reason? Do we uplift those around us by working to be a team player with integrity, or do we only fulfill the bare minimum in order to get a paycheck?

# JEALOUS & ENVIOUS LOVE

James 3:14-16AMP:

*"But if you are bitterly jealous and there is selfish ambition in your heart, don't cover up the truth with boasting and lying. For jealousy and selfishness are not God's kind of wisdom. Such things are earthly, unspiritual, and demonic. For where jealousy and selfish ambition exist, there will be disorder and every vile practice."*

Jealousy is the fear of losing something and envy is a resentful desire to have something another enjoys. In order for jealousy to even be birthed, there must be a sense of competition. Similarly, envy comes from a place of discontentment based on the perception that someone lives a better life than you. Beloved, it does you no good to be jealous or envious of your neighbor, just as it does them no good to have those same inclinations about you. Television shows like Fatal Attraction and Lifetime stories have given us visuals of the progression of jealousy and envy, and their power to turn everyday people into thieves and murderers. Love is suffocated in an atmosphere of jealousy, and jealousy leads to mischief and excitement over the downfall of others. Given all of this, we arrive at the probing question: "Why do believers try to ignite jealousy and envy within others?" Let's be honest, sometimes we want others to covet what we have and feel threatened by us. We want people to exalt us and feed into our egos. However, this competitiveness and sense of self-importance brings God no glory.

In 1 Corinthians 13, we are shown that love does not envy or boast, nor is it arrogant. Instigating jealousy, envy, and competition are all done out of arrogant pride. The love you give can never be unconditional if you consistently post on social media for the sole purpose of provoking covetousness from your neighbor. Examine your motives to identify why you feel the need to compete with others. What is about them that threatens you? You should raise this same question in any moments in which you feel envy or jealousy toward another. What is it that ignites those feelings of jealousy? Is it their wardrobe, achievements, marriage, their God given platform?

Beloved, God graces you for a path and graces another for a different path. You cannot thrive in love and at the same time harbor jealousy for God's gifts to His creation. When you find yourself feeling jealous or envious of another, I challenge you to confess those feelings to God. Choose to pray for that person and praise God for what He is doing in their lives. I challenge you to declare that God continue to bless them financially, declare they are the head and not the tail, and declare they have more than enough and will bear fruit in their season. I challenge you beloved, to declare that they will continue to thrive. Praying when jealousy and envy rise up acts as a guard to prevent you feeling threatened and acting on that jealousy as Cain did, when he killed Abel. This level of honesty and maturity brings God glory.

*Competition that does not elevate is toxic and taints love.*

# I'M IN MY FEELINGS...

A person gets offended when they feel attacked, disrespected, or when their pride is hurt. I've had the displeasure of witnessing how often we believers get offended due to hypersensitivity, even when being told the truth. In the church, there are too many nerve centers that are easily struck. At times, the offense we feel is warranted, specifically if we are wrongly disrespected by another. Nevertheless, the Bible never called us to demand respect, but rather to show it. Likewise, the Bible never called us to demand love, it requires us to demonstrate it.

Throughout my pregnancy, I was very prone to offense. I was hypersensitive and therefore quick to anger because I perceived comments or suggestions from others as an attack, and made myself ready for war at any time. Eventually, I found myself telling my husband that I needed to back away from certain people. The problem with backing away is that it translated into not going to church or other events and being mentally absent in the presence of others. My desire to retreat also meant that I avoided serving in ministry and stopped responding to phone messages because I did not want my self-control tested. In hindsight, I realize that there's a difference between being offended and taking offense. In my heart, I knew that I was choosing to take offense. It became clear that the comments made toward me during that time were mainly innocent and that people's treatment of me typically had nothing to do with me individually. For my offence to be justified, I would've had to experience actual verbal or physical attack, and that was not the case.

This experience revealed to me that more often than not, we take offense when we're not actually being offended, and we often wrongly handle our responses to those situations. We take a situation that could be handled privately and make it gossip by reporting it to our sister or brother, cousin, best friend or anyone who will listen. When we feel the need to constantly recount a moment of offense, we aren't looking for anything but the validation for our reaction. We make it a public spectacle by venting on social media so that we can unload that story on yet another person who might cosign our anger and offense. As an example, I recall a specific social media post from young Christian woman who vented her thoughts about her unexpected pregnancy, which stirred gossip and judgement from others. Instead of individually addressing those comments with the people who wrote them, she took to social media to discuss how she was being judged and ridiculed. After reading her post, I examined her comments section and saw over 30 comments from others who co-signed her anger by telling her that her actions were okay, that only God can judge her, and that she should leave her church.

What would our lives begin to look like if at every moment that we took offense to the comment of another, we went directly to that person in a loving manner and admitted how those words hurt us? What if every time we were offended or we took offense, we prayed for God to change our hearts and minds, to give us the strength to love that person even deeper with the love of Christ?

It serves us no purpose to gossip to our neighbor about our problems with another. In Colossians 3, the Bible advises us not to lie to each other and to speak directly to our brother or sister if there is any offense between us (Matt 18:15). So if the Bible tells us how to handle conflict and feelings, why do we involve outside individuals in the conflict? After becoming a mother, I noticed how much more sensitive and irritable I felt and found myself constantly complaining to my sisters about others. One day, a thought in my spirit hit me like a ton of bricks: "Why am I trying to control and change people as though I am Jesus? Whose fault is it that I am offended by their words? Instead of helping the offender to be a better person, does it make me feel any better to vent to my sisters and taint their vision of that individual?"

I had to pray for God to change me. I allowed offense to creep in when I should have brought my thoughts into captivity under the obedience of Jesus Christ. Moreover, my reactions proved I needed to toughen up. I cannot walk in unconditional love and forgiveness if I am so easily enslaved by offense. Daily, I would pray for God to change my heart and allow me to speak my truth, while standing up for myself in a way that was still respectful and loving. It is important that everyone has the time and space to vent to when needed, but not everything needs to be vented to another human. As much as I wanted to, as a believer and someone who aspires to walk worthy of this call (Eph 4:1), I realized that cannot choose to cut people off just because I don't want to forgive them over words, especially words that don't threaten my life or my salvation.

Have you ever met someone who was so filled with the Christian spirit that they continuously opened their hearts to offer a prayer or plate of food even to those who gossiped about them? I have an aunt who embodies this spirit. Even when she is hurt by another, she prays for the perpetrator, and if she needs to, she will express her hurt feelings to a trusted family member. After that expression of pain is released, she no longer mentions the issue or acts any differently towards the individual (unless instructed by God to distance herself). What a way to be, right? She never surrenders her peace to the perpetrator or allows herself to be a victim. Instead, she chooses to make the decision to stand on God's charge of love and forgiveness, so that she will always be victorious. In her eyes, it is worth more to honor God than it is to be caught up in offense or revenge. When you surrender your peace to offense over minor things, you decide not to be victorious. Alternatively, you decide to be a victim and the enemy relishes in your victimization. He knows that as long as you are offended, you are not loving, peaceful, or forgiving. How can we expect to be forgiven if we do not forgive? "For if you forgive other people when they sin again you, your heavenly Father will also forgive you (Matthew 6:14 NIV)"

Ephesians 4:2-3 tells us, "With all humility and gentleness, with patience, bearing with one another in love, eager to maintain the unity of the Spirit in the bond of peace." In other words, be excited about keeping the peace, even if that means you have to take the loss. That's not to say that you should allow people to run over you. In these situations, we should always default to prayer – I firmly believe in consulting with Jesus when I feel the need to cut ties with certain people. The Bible even has guidelines for the types of people who should only be your acquaintances in life. However, be determined not to make your neighbor an outcast. As frustrating as people can be, you can still help to bear their burdens in wisdom and love on people like crazy. We should attempt to exemplify the words found in 1 Peter 2:23: "When he was reviled, he did not revile in return; when he suffered, he did not threaten, but continued entrusting himself to him who judges justly." The scripture is clear. In those moments when offense is creeping upon you, and people are irritating you to the point that you are ready to take off the Lord Jesus Christ, entrust them to God by withholding the 'beat your face in' verbal retaliation that you really want to give.

Want to know something crazy? I used to rehearse my come backs to different offensive things (it's okay to laugh, it's funny). I would stand in the mirror and say out loud the things that would offend me if someone said it and then calculate exactly how I would retaliate so as to publicly wound them and ensure any spectators were on my side at the end of it all. Beloved, we are human, we get offended, and we offend. But, we are also believers and this must trump our animal instincts to savagely defend and retaliate. Parenting our emotions is one of life's great challenges, but it must be done in order to give God the glory. We must strive to live as Jesus lived, we must take people's salvation more personal than their offensive behavior, and we must take our peace more personal than any desires for revenge. When we choose peace over offense, we let our light shine before men and God is honored.

## SANDPAPER

Prayerfully today we would be discerning enough to recognize the sandpaper in our lives (the people and situations that work our last nerves)! May we be more concerned with God's development of our character than we are with creating circumstances that make us feel more comfortable, but cause us to shine less brilliantly as a result. I pray we choose to be polished today, so that when God looks at us, He sees Himself in us.

Amen.

# MODERN DAY PHARISEE IN ME?

The older I get, the more I realize that Pharisees still exist today. The first instance I recognized this was within myself. If you are familiar with the Pharisees, you may know that the Pharisees did not teach Christianity. In fact, they did not even believe Jesus was the Son of God, even when He performed miracles. The Pharisees opposed the very message of Christ by their lifestyle, beliefs, and the righteous indignation they embodied. It was always very clear that Jesus Himself was at odds with the Pharisees, considering they always questioned His religious integrity because his disciples did not practice strict obedience to the rules. Jesus' disciples healed on the Sabbath, picked grain on the Sabbath (see Mark 2:23-27), nor did they fast like the Pharisees did (see Mark 2:18). Jesus ate with "unclean" people and the Pharisees were just not down for that (Luke 15:1-2).

Today, our churches are inundated by Pharisaical

Christians. These modern-day Pharisees conduct their lives with the mindset that abiding by all of the rules will give them the key to heaven and they impose that same philosophy on others striving toward Christ. We know very well that we are saved by GRACE, not works (Eph 2:8-9). Even if you have kept every single commandment and have a spotless record in the eyes of man, you cannot be saved unless you have accepted Jesus Christ. The point is, Christianity is about a RELATIONSHIP, <u>not</u> MINDLESS RULE-FOLLOWING!

Today the behavior of the Pharisees is evident when you enter churches and face condemnation from people for every possible thing: the length of your skirt, the earrings in your ears, your diet, your hairstyle, your job, being a single parent, your infrequent Bible study attendance. The list could go on and on. There are people, maybe in every church, that are busy beating others over the head with rules for how they must conduct their lives in order to be accepted into heaven. I understand that people must be warned of the dangers of sin, but when believers begin to call down hell's brimstone and fire on others, it is evident that they have been infected with the Pharisee's "yeast" (Matt 16:6).

Personally, if I am not careful, I can create a warm and moist atmosphere for the yeast of the Pharisees to activate. As a result, I will find myself doing things for the outward projection of religion. Therefore, my example became permission for others to follow after religion and completely neglect their need for relationship. If you take a look at Matthew 23:23-24, you'll see that Jesus told the Pharisees that they tithed religiously but forgot the more important matters, like justice, MERCY, and faithfulness. Inside of all of us, maybe there is a little packet of "Religious Pharisee Yeast" waiting to be opened, but we must keep it closed by the power of the Holy Spirit.

People run away from Christ because Christianity seems to revolve around following a bunch of rules in order to avoid damnation. In reality, Christianity is beautifully and uniquely ONLY about a reciprocating love between Father and child (Matt 28:9, Ps 68:5, Is 63:16), Husband and Wife (Is 54:5), and Bride and Bridegroom (Rev 19:7). If we always saw our relationship with Christ as just that – a RELATIONSHIP –then imagine how our view of Christianity would change. We would come to know His love and just be burning to introduce others to that love so that they too can experience the beauty of Christ. Since it was love that sent Christ to Calvary's cross, wouldn't it also be love that causes us to do what pleases the Bridegroom so that we can be in eternal love with Him in heaven? If we are waiting for the Bridegroom we love so deeply, shouldn't we be busy preparing for His arrival (Luke 19:13), especially knowing that He left to prepare a place for us (John 14:3)?

It is time to do away with our inner Pharisees. people do not come to church to be beat down with more rules, life has already placed a stranglehold on them. Church and Christians should be conduits of Christ's LOVE, reflecting relationship not mindless rule following. As a wife, I do many things JUST BECAUSE they please my husband, in spite of any feelings I may have. I invest time learning what makes his joy extra full, what will add a smile to his face, and what will help to make our home peaceful for him. I do all of these things because I LOVE HIM AND I WANT TO DEMONSTRATE THAT LOVE IN A WAY THAT IS RECOGNIZABLE TO HIM! You might be familiar with a book called *The 5 Love Languages*, by Gary Chapman which is a self-help book describing how to effectively communicate love within relationships. Jesus has a love language of His own, which He tells us is "LOVE GOD AND ONE ANOTHER!" Look with me to Matthew 22:37-40 AMP:

"And Jesus replied to him, 'You shall love the Lord your God with all your heart, and with all your soul, and with all your mind.' This is the first and greatest commandment. The second is like it, 'You shall love your neighbor as yourself [that is, unselfishly seek the best or higher good for others].'"

Let us remember Revelation 2:4 (KJV), in which Jesus said the church at Ephesus had done everything right, but the indictment against them was simple, "You have left your first love." I love how the New Living Translation (NLT) illustrates this message "But I have this complaint against you. You don't love me or each other as you did at first!" We all know what happens in a marriage when the love is gone. Eventually, if nothing is done then divorce is soon to come. Pharisee-ism implies a loveless relationship with God and our neighbors. Modern day Pharisee-ism is a demonstration of love for God through mindless obedience based in the false concept that heaven is earned. When in reality, I believe in our spiritual marriage we must demonstrate love for God and Christ by loving each other and mindfully doing what pleases Him because we care about Him.

I don't want to give you the misconception that you will love to do everything that pleases God and embodies being a good neighbor. Your faith will be tested when you have to forgive difficult people, love on those who hate, and hold your peace in the midst of having your character dragged through the mud. However, why else would you do it? Let me tell you why…It is because love for Him has been awakened inside of you and it responds to the love He demonstrated when Jesus hung cursed and forsaken on the cross of Calvary. God has done everything to show us the extent of His love, a love that has been proven time and time again. The love that awakens inside of us for Him causes us to demonstrate love in return.

There is no relationship in mindless rule-following, just rebellion. When my mother's reason for me to do something I deemed bizarre was "Because I said so", it fueled rebellion in me and made me never want to do it again. However, there was a time when she demanded something of me and told me the reason – because she loved me and wanted the best for me. Hearing this made me want to do it just to please her, because I understood her heart. Do not allow yourself to be a Pharisee who tells people to obey the rules in the Bible so God won't kill them. And, don't be a mindless rule follower trying to buy your way into heaven. Seek to be a genuine believer pursuing relationship and deeper love. Active curiosity feeds our enthusiasm and passion for Christ. If we keep feeding that curiosity with prayer, looking to The Word, and living The Word by the power of the Holy Spirit, there is no way we could ever mindlessly follow the rules. Be warned though, you might end up hopefully in love!

If we look at the scriptures, we will find that God is a romantic. Take a look at the way He talked about Israel, at the way He kept fighting for her, and the way He fought for us through the life, death, and resurrection of Christ. Look at how He fights for us daily when He grants us life anew, and blesses us beyond anything we could ever even begin to deserve. He loves us so deeply. He is wooing us even now…can't you see it? Wooing us and wanting us to respond by loving Him and loving others, and letting the pure love keep us on the path of righteousness.

Can you see it?...

This new era of Pharisee-ism is partially to blame for our state of broken down Christianity. We can't just get with the program because the program is designed to promote our slavery to rules instead of liberty in relationship. Some of us who have been broken down but remained Christians, have in turn used the same system to break others down; can we stop already? Loving your neighbor as yourself is to do the opposite of the Pharisees as told by Jesus in Matthew 23:15 AMP, "Woe to you, [self-righteous] scribes and Pharisees, hypocrites, because you travel over sea and land to make a single proselyte (convert to Judaism), and when he becomes a convert, you make him twice as much a son of hell as you are." Loving our neighbors in response to loving God means we help to make people's experience of God and His love better than when we first encountered them.

# DON'T COUNT ME OUT

*Now there was a believer in Damascus named Ananias. The Lord spoke to him in a vision, calling, "Ananias!"*

*"Yes, Lord!" he replied.*

*The Lord said, 'Go over to Straight Street, to the house of Judas. When you get there, ask for a man from Tarsus named Saul. He is praying to me right now. I have shown him a vision of a man named Ananias coming in and laying hands on him so he can see again.'*

*"But Lord," exclaimed Ananias, "I've heard many people talk about the terrible things this man has done to the believers in Jerusalem! And he is authorized by the leading priests to*

*arrest everyone who calls upon your name."*

*But the Lord said, 'Go, for Saul is my chosen instrument to take my message to the Gentiles and to kings, as well as to the people of Israel. And I will show him how much he must suffer for my name's sake.'*

*So Ananias went and found Saul. He laid his hands on him and said, "Brother Saul, the Lord Jesus..."* Acts 9:10-17 NLT

We do not have the right to count anyone out! The very one you fear sharing the gospel with and refuse to pray for may be God's chosen instrument! Thankfully, even though humans will attempt to disqualify others due to their past, God does the qualifying. But beautifully, God redeems us and repurposes that past for His glory and for the benefit of others' eternity. Choosing to count someone out by not praying for them, helping to meet their needs, or fearing them is not beneficial to anyone. Fearing someone to the point of cowardice means you invest more time in avoiding them than you do sharing Jesus and showing them His heart at work in you. You have to ask yourself, "Am I selectively kind, compassionate, and forgiving? Or am I choosing to purposely withhold the gospel from this person because I fear their opinion?" And this includes the unsaved friends we don't share the gospel with. God is not on vacation...He chooses who gets to hear about Jesus with the charge "Go ye into the world and preach the gospel to every creature" (Matt 16:15).

We do not have the right to count people out of salvation! We do not have the right to determine that someone is beyond hope when it comes to Christianity! Salvation is not ours to give; and the love, kindness, forgiveness, and compassion of Jesus Christ are not ours to withhold. Do not misunderstand me please – your personal life and who you cut out of it is not relevant to this discussion. This is about withholding the gospel because of your feelings about someone's reputation. Everyone has an invitation to Jesus Christ, and YOU AS A CHRISTIAN ARE THE INVITATION DELIVERER! It may be your prayer that brings healing in their life, or it may be your compassion that heals their broken heart. It may be your expressions of love, or your sharing of the gospel that causes them to be saved. Even if someone is a *no-good*, manipulating, trifling human being, they have a right to hear the gospel, and you do not have a right to withhold it. Furthermore, when you are led by the Holy Spirit to address them, it must be with respect, in the same manner that Ananias addressed Saul as "Brother Saul". Your disobedience is a hindrance to their salvation! You make yourself responsible for their delayed repentance. Please note that I am talking to myself first because I have been convicted by these exact words as I wrote them. Let's mature! Let's correctly represent Jesus!

# JOURNAL ENTRY: SELF-RIGHTEOUS AND SELF-SERVING

*Today Nelson Mandela, affectionately known as Madiba died and I cried. I saw Madiba as my great grandfather, his legacy meant more to me than I had the wisdom to understand. The world's iconic black men are dying, and it doesn't bother me that I never had a chance to meet him, it bothers me that we have one less African man with a character saturated in beauty who was willing to risk it all for everyone else. We need more role models, a remnant of those great men who were ready to die for our sakes. I loved Madiba, a man I never knew and never saw beyond the television and magazines, but I was mentally attached to his character.*

*It made me question myself not naturally but spiritually, and I asked myself: "Are you ready to be imprisoned for 20 years to help others find Christ? Can you give up your dreams of various degrees, annual summer vacations, and designer clothing to fight the cause of Christ if that is what God requires?"*

*You see, my lessons from Madiba are not about racial equality, but spiritual freedom. Am I a bystander to my brother's soul-sabotage or will I stand up for his freedom through intercession, fasting, and helping supply His need? Will I gossip about my sister's wardrobe or will I go to the store and gift her with more appropriate yet stylish clothes? Will I watch my sister prostitute herself to feed her children or will I take the groceries from my own home and give it to her secretly? Souls are at risk, and are being oppressed by some of us who call ourselves Christians.*

Too many Christians have come to a point where they believe they are better than another because they have been saved longer, forgetting that they too once lived the same lifestyle and were immature Christians. Instead of using the testimony to bring someone closer to Christ, they encourage separation in the church by refusing to reach out in love to those whose souls need saving and whose walk with Christ needs maturing. It is essential to remember that not only did Christ come for the lost to be redeemed (Luke 19:10), but, He came to SEEK THEM OUT in order to redeem them. So the question now is, as a believer, are you available for Christ to seek the lost through your words, attitudes and actions?

For a long time, I struggled to like *church people*. I'd never encountered so many gossiping, backbiting, and cruel people in my life. I thank God that when my mom died, He placed me in a ministry where loving on each other and the community was of great importance. My Pastor, Dr. R, boldly shared her testimony in the community. Wednesday nights she could be found playing dominos with the people, making

Jesus a part of every aspect of the conversation. Dr. R would take the Sunday offerings, buy groceries, and put them on the altar for anyone who needed to come and take. She was never afraid to get involved with people for the cause of Christ, and because of this we followed suit. Every Wednesday we spent time out in the community interacting with those around us in ways that inspired them to attend prayer meetings and want to know more about Christ.

*In eternity, there will be separation between the saved and those who rejected Christ. We are not there yet, but don't you want to love as many people toward Christ as is possible? If Nelson Mandela was a preacher, I strongly believe that his approach to ministry would be loving people into the liberty of Jesus Christ. Don't ever forget this, don't become so busy chasing happiness that you leave destitute the souls depending on your genuine obedience to God's call on your life. Don't become so comfortable just attending church on Sunday, that you forget to leave the four walls and go seek people out.*

I am in no way chastising anyone, I too have my own faults. I have been known to not talk to people just because I didn't like the way they spoke. This message is for me too, I have got to be a better sister and love extravagantly. While there may be people we do not like, we are commanded to make the choice to love everyone through the demonstration of the attributes of Christ and the fruits of the spirit. This doesn't mean that we need to keep harmful people in our lives, loving some people may also mean detaching yourself for the benefit of you both. After all, you should not maintain close attachments to those who blatantly disrespect your relationship with Christ and continually put you in tempting situations.

Even so, you as a Christian are obligated to extend the very same grace, love, mercy, and peace Christ extended to you when He came and sought you out before redemption. How can we say that we love Christ, but treat people like pariahs because of their appearance? I have been a firsthand witness to Christians turning people away from the church because of earrings, clothes, and the food they choose to eat. I am not saying you should advocate for skimpy attire and unhealthy eating, but if you can't see past an individual's outward appearance, then YOU are the one in trouble. Look at the example of Jonah (Jonah 4:1-4), he ended up in the belly of the fish because he decided that the people of Ninevah were unworthy of forgiveness again. That type of rebellion and merciless judgement still rears its ugly head in many Christians today. You decide that others are unworthy of the gospel that should be shared with them, and the example of Christ that should be demonstrated to them through you. Therefore, you make it harder for them to be won over (Proverbs 18:19). God can use someone else to win that soul in time, but what will be the reason you give Him for why you chose not to.

Family, we must SNAP OUT OF THE SELF-RIGHTEOUSNESS! Recognize that you are not without sin, which is why you need Jesus every day. That's why we must die to self every day, not just one day once and for all. Cover your brother and sister in love, not insults and gossip. Win them over with your honesty, gentleness, and compassion; don't lose them with eye-rolling and nasty facial expressions of rudeness. What will you tell Jesus when He asks you about how you treated sister so-and-so because her skirt was not long enough, her hair was purple, or because she praised in a way that made you uncomfortable? There were times I myself sat in church too distracted by someone's lack of a jacket to appreciate that they were pouring their heart out in worship to God. Crazy right? Instead of engaging in the corporate worship, I sat there judging my fellow Christian sister (who was known to have a drink and club on a Saturday and be back in church on Sunday morning) as she surrendered to Christ. Instead of seeing the sincerity of her worship, all I could see was that she was worshipping without a jacket and that her armpits were visible. My goodness, I was a complete mess of a Christian. Lord, please clean me up and keep me from becoming that person ever again.

# A PRAYER FOR US

Oh Sweet Jesus, we are so far from what we ought to be, but we are thankful that when You come we shall be like You. In the meantime, Oh Lord, we struggle to walk like we are worthy, we struggle to act on the truth that whatever we do to others we have done unto You. If I am honest, there is a child in me crying out, "Why can't we just get it right! Why do we keep misrepresenting You to the world?" Help us, please deliver us from ourselves, and grant us more opportunities to share the gospel, and to be kind and generous to others. For all the times we have failed to prove trustworthy with this great assignment, please forgive us. Awaken a burning desire within us to love our neighbors, to love them so much that we would pursue them with forgiveness, kindness, grace, fellowship, and love as the Holy Spirit leads. Cause us to be our brothers' keepers, praying for them instead of succumbing to the temptation to gossip, and help us not to taint people's visions of others by sharing their past mistakes. Lord, when we find ourselves face to face with offense, may we choose compassion and mercy instead of anger. Today, make our tongues tools and not weapons, inviting people to experience grace, encouragement, the gospel of Jesus Christ, and appreciation by our actions and words. May we reserve judgement for ourselves and pour out extravagant grace for others.

Amen.

# BROKE DOWN CHRISTIANS

# 3

# BROKE DOWN HEART

# HEART MATTERS

Growing up, I was always pushed to "follow my heart" in every area of my life, especially where my future was concerned. Beloved, do you know that I was being incorrectly conditioned? The wisdom of this world continues to conflict with the wisdom of God, and that is perfectly fine, I was just ill-prepared to experience this conflict in my own life. You see, if I had followed my heart, I would have missed many opportunities. For one, I would have gone to graduate school with my scholarship instead of following God's path. You might be thinking, "Shonda, you're a Christian, surely your heart told you to do what God wanted." I can promise you that it did not. The heart will tell you to do what makes you feel good or what is good, but good is not always Godly! Jeremiah 17:9 AMP says "The heart is deceitful above all things and it is extremely sick; Who can understand it fully *and* know its secret motives?"

At this point one has to pause and ask, "Well doesn't God know my heart? He knows I'm trying to be a better Christian and stop clubbing and drinking but sometimes..." Yes, beloved, God does know your heart and that's why Jeremiah 17:9 was written. He knows it is extremely sick, the NLT says "and desperately wicked." "Desperately wicked" means the heart looks for ways to sin, it craves wickedness. You may not even be aware that what you are doing is sinful sometimes, but following your heart and not the Holy Spirit causes you to commit indeliberate sins. The first clause in Jeremiah 17:9 tells us nothing is more deceitful than the heart, and this is the very reason that believers go around repeating the phrase "God knows my heart". If you are bound in a cycle of sin, you can easily be deceived by your own heart to believe your behavior is acceptable to God. This innate deceitfulness is also why James 1:6-8 NLT is true in our lives:

"But when you ask Him, be sure that your faith is in God alone. Do not waver, for a person with divided loyalty is as unsettled as a wave of the sea that is blown and tossed by the wind. Such people should not expect to receive anything from the Lord. Their loyalty is divided between God and the world, and they are unstable in everything they do."

Loyalty is a response to kindness that begins in the heart. The Bible teaches that David was a man after God's own heart (1 Sam 13:14). He was loyal to God, but the moment he found himself stealing another man's wife and committing ungodly murder, he was following his own deceptive and desperately wicked heart, not God's.

A great deal of our experience with David is repentance. This is one of the keys, I believe, that made him a man after

God's own heart. Psalm 51:7-10 expresses this point so beautifully:

"Purify me from my sins, and I will be clean; wash me, and I will be whiter than snow. Oh, give me back my joy again; you have broken me— now let me rejoice. Don't keep looking at my sins. Remove the stain of my guilt. Create in me a clean heart, O God. Renew a loyal spirit within me."

The pursuit of God's heart begins with repentance. Although David repented poetically, you and I just need to repent honestly. We cannot begin to cultivate loyalty toward God by following our desperately wicked hearts. Even Paul, who saw Jesus with his own two eyes, struggled with doing good and did the evil that he didn't want to do (Rom 7:19-20). I know that we use the scripture "foolishness is bound in the heart of a child (Prov 22:15)" to express why children are disciplined, but remember that we are also God's children, so foolishness is interwoven in our hearts. I sincerely hope I haven't lost you, but the logic is simple: If your heart is desperately wicked, deceitful, and foolish, why follow it? It does not make spiritual or natural sense.

So what's the next step Shonda? We need to repent as honestly as David did, and pray daily for God to create in us a clean heart and a loyal spirit. We need to become more discerning of the Holy Spirit, so we can know heart from head and therefore maneuver away from opportunities to sin whether deliberate or otherwise. If you search yourself, you will find you have a history of deception from your own heart. The heart is so deceiving that when you sin it tells you to hide from the only One who can clean you up. When you get offended at church, the heart tells you not to go back, but the church experience is necessary for your healing and empowerment toward Christ. When you break up with a man you know was wrong for you, your heart will tell you to keep checking his social media and to "keep in touch". This prevents you from moving on, and doesn't cause a renewal of the relationship, just a renewal of fornication. You know it's the truth beloved, I KNOW it's the truth and experience is on my side. The heart is so messed up it makes you harden yourself to the very things and people designed to help and refine you. You go around lying that you're fine and everything is okay but every time you even think about that person or that experience you become overwhelmed by powerful, harmful emotions.

A hardened heart cannot obey the will of God, especially if it is not in the best interest of one's mortality. A hardened heart will go to church, hear the message, feel no conviction, and go away unchanged. A hardened heart will cause you to laugh at the present pain of others, encourage rejection, and push people away from Christ. This is why your heart cannot lead you, because it has a strong desire to defend itself and preserve the ego. A heart led by Christ, however, flowing in the heart of Christ Himself, focuses on eternity, doing the will of God, and service to others. No egos are serviced when the heart submits to Christ, only more glory is given to God and you lay up for yourself treasures in heaven. Is this not a part of why we are broken down? Our hearts are caught up in natural (rather than spiritual) self-preservation as we service our egos and emotions, rather than in serving the purposes of Christ. There is a little bit wrong with every one of us Christians – some of us have a lot of mess to work out or a lot of broken pieces to get through. But no matter how tall the pile of garbage, it all needs to be cleaned up. That clean-up starts in the heart.

After repentance, you need to get into the Word, for it is the very discerner of the thoughts and intents of the heart (Heb 4:12-13 AMP). It will equip you with the tools needed to manage yourself, and help you understand when the Holy Spirit is leading you so that your trust in God can grow. Beloved, you cannot trust the heart, it is the Holy Spirit living on the inside that must be trusted. They are not the same. The Holy Spirit will guide you into all truth (Rom 2:5), the heart alone will guide you right into hell. When the heart is contaminated it channels everything that hinders life, specifically a thriving life in Christ. Where do you think Sister Judgmental gets her critical and depressing attitude from, always having something negative to say but never any solutions to the so-called problems she points out? Proverbs 6:14 AMP tells us that a "perverted heart devises evil, continually sowing discord." Likewise Matthew 15:19 NLT says, "from the heart come evil thoughts, murder, adultery, all sexual immorality, theft, lying, and slander. This is why the Bible tells us to "watch over your heart with all diligence, for from it flows the springs of life (Prov 4:23 AMP)."

Bible study, prayer, fasting, and church fellowship (GO TO CHURCH BELOVED) will help keep your heart oriented to God's heart. I know you're probably thinking that I just made a big deal out of one saying, and you would be right – the heart is the biggest deal there is. When I said the prayer of repentance, I uttered the words "Lord Jesus, come into my heart." My heart was the first place that I invited Jesus in my life, and I didn't invite Him in to just be a guest but to demolish, and rebuild anew. You invited Christ into your heart also, He was there knocking and you answered. Now you face the daily challenge of choosing to follow your dilapidated deceitful heart or Christ's pure heart into God's eternal rest for us. When our hearts flow in God's, life won't break us and we won't be bound in cycles of sin. Instead, we will break in worship and be continually transformed. I want to stress the need for repentance and honesty, it all begins with the truth. Pour from yourself everything that is in your heart before God and watch Him honor your honesty by changing your heart.

Beloved, "today if you hear His voice, harden not your heart (Heb 3:15 KJV)."

# A PRAYER FOR US

Lord God, the truth is, we are wretched, we have been disloyal, and therefore we are unstable. We struggle to live in Your will, to even love ourselves because we are busy following our toxic hearts. Your word has revealed that foolishness is bound in our hearts. Your word has revealed that our hearts are a fountain of life or death. We chose life today, we choose to guard our hearts by studying and living Your word. Even as we make these choices, let Your word divide from us the deceitful desires in our hearts. Let Your word be our guard rail as we practice living it out. God, our hearts have led us into some deep pits of sin, so as You forgive us cause us to forgive ourselves and release the past into Your care. Our hearts want to hold onto all the pain and anger we've stored up in them, but empty us out Oh God. Come into our hearts and transform our lives so that we can go forth in Your heart and help to transform the lives of others.

Amen.

# BELIEF

As I explored one of the many reasons that I was in a broken down state as a Christian, I realized that I had a belief issue. I happily quoted scriptures that I had committed to memory, but never truly believed them. Philippians 4:13 NLT, "I can do all things through Christ, who gives me strength" and Romans 8:37 NLT, "Despite all these things, overwhelming victory is ours through Christ, who loves us" were frequently on my lips but seldom blossoming in my heart and mind. When I was a newlywed Christian, my belief in God's word seemed to be like an impenetrable wall. I used to be fully convinced that I could do all things through Christ, that in Him I was more than a conqueror and He would supply my every need. As I grew up in age, my belief dwindled.

The summer after I graduated from college, I was broke and annoyed at my empty bank account. I would tell myself God was going to work it out but I would stress, work up an ungodly appetite, and dehydrate myself crying trying to figure out a solution in case God didn't come through for me. I actually thought God's plan A needed a plan B and C for support. I was so fed up waiting on God for my financial breakthrough that I took a job without praying, and got to stand on my feet for over 12 hours daily, ending up too tired to even study the Word when I got back home, let alone go to church. Seriously beloved, the job had absolutely no chairs, no desks, not even a lunch room. I also didn't have a car to sit in which meant I had to wait an additional hour standing to be picked up. My problem was that I could do all things through Christ except wait on God for guidance with regard to my employment status and finances. I could do all things through Christ except wisely handle the refund checks I received in school to ensure that I had funds during the summer after graduation. *Ouch*!

The same applies to too many Christians. We don't truly believe many of the verses we quote, and we fail to realize or acknowledge that people are always watching us. Beloved, the physical and emotional responses you have to temptations, pressure, pain, and especially to scripture, influence those around you to not only judge your Christianity, but to decide that Jesus has limitations. How can we expect anyone to follow us to Christ when we struggle to believe God will perform His will? When we respond to problems in the same way that the world responds, those who watch us don't see any reason to believe in the Jesus we claim to know because our responses are no different than anyone else's.

It is an unfortunate truth that many Christians seem to only be able to do certain things through Christ – such as earning degrees and increasing income – but somehow can't stop gossiping. Some Christians can even endure the financially dry season while tightly holding onto God's promises, but cannot stop fornicating. Beloved, if you can do ALL THINGS through Christ, it also means you can stop committing sexual sin, using your tongue for evil, and hiding iniquity in your heart. You can learn to accept criticism and mature, and thereby learn to return a kind word for ill treatment. If you truly can do ALL THINGS through Christ, then you can stop squandering money and then begging for help to pay bills, and you can stop acting in pride and jealousy off of Instagram pictures. Through Christ you can develop healthy eating habits and self-care so that you will not be bogged down by sickness and can do His work. Think about it, how can any Christian claim to be empowered by Christ to do ALL things, but live like Christ's power is not enough to change habitual sinful ways?

You know I am talking to us right? The very reason we are Broke Down Christians is because our belief in Christ is conditional. The impact of church in our lives is limited and the guidance of the Holy Spirit on critical issues goes ignored whenever we disagree with the direction. The very reason we are broken down is because we have spiritual issues that manifest mentally (disobedience, lack of motivation, lack of conviction), physically (fornication, gluttony, disease from poor habits, disobedience), and emotionally (unkindness, unforgiveness, judgment, hatred).

Belief is not in the tongue at all, only confession is in the tongue. Belief lies in the heart and is proven in the actions. Be encouraged to believe God in this season and forever. We can heap up good works, we can pray in many tongues, we can fast for days. But, if we don't believe God beloved, then we have no right to expect anything from Him (James 1:6-8).

# SURRENDER

*I am in charge of my surrender!*

The surrender is mine to give, and the only person always hindering my surrender to love, life, adventure, success, peace, and trust...is me! I am desperately in charge of my surrender, and although I claim that God is in control of my life, I am in charge of how much control He has.

I believe He is a rewarder of them that diligently seek Him, but the diligence is mine to embody. I believe He will give me the desires of my heart when I please Him, but the degree to which my life brings Him pleasure is mine to determine. I am totally and completely in charge of my surrender. So I make this effort every day to fully surrender to the life that is before me; surrender to the creativity, LOVE, peace, and adventure that align with God's will. I make a powerful effort to surrender to the hurt, sorrow, and tears orchestrated to mature me, so that I may *be subject to all the rainbows & beauty of life in Jesus Christ.*

*My failure to surrender is what holds me hostage. Refusal to surrender my concept of self, money, love, relationships, and work hinders me from being limitless. It hinders me from experiencing the ALL THINGS I say I can do through Christ Jesus.*

I talk about surrender in this way because I observe with awe how the world (non-Christians) has surrendered to Biblical principles and found success, love, and peace (obviously not Jesus' peace). They are able to build generational wealth, write bestselling novels, and help others overcome mammoth-sized emotional and spiritual issues WITHOUT EVEN KNOWING JESUS! Look at Instagram, how many more people are surrendering to health by cutting out red meat, becoming vegan, making better food choices, going dairy or gluten free, or becoming vegetarian? Go into your churches, how many people are sick with food-related illnesses including obesity and hypertension? Go into your church and see how many people are faithfully tithing BUT still living pay-check to pay-check, have zero savings and/or are on welfare? How is it that people who do not even acknowledge Jesus Christ as Lord and Savior can enact the financial and mental (thinking, believing, professing) principles of The Word of God and at the least have financial stability BUT we believers REFUSE to surrender to God's Word and live it out? HOW?!!! We have refused to believe the Word of God is profitable in every area of our lives, and I speak with such conviction about this because the evidence is in our bank accounts, our work ethic, our attitude, our envy of other's success, our failure to read, and our hatred of correction.

Surrender to living The Word of God. As more people are opting for entrepreneurship, there seems to be discussion about the wealth of millionaires and the multiple streams of income they utilize to remain profitable. Beloved, do you know that this principle is derived from Ecclesiastes 11:2? Go read it beloved, it's in there. The Bible tells you to have several business ventures, give generously, secure an inheritance for your children, and work hard but smart. How is it that we go to church Monday, Wednesday, Friday, Saturday, and Sunday where pastors are preaching the same Bible that tells you how to become prosperous, yet we are living as emotional, spiritual, physical, and financial paupers? How?

Beloved, in many areas we aren't lacking and "going through," because it is God's will, but because we are truthfully lazy, complacent, and irresponsible. We hate work even though before God gave Adam a companion and helpmate, He gave Adam work. We live by words only, and we refuse to surrender the words to the feet and let them become one. You can declare and decree victory all you want but never forget James 2:17 faith without works is dead and Matthew 7:20 you will be recognized by your fruits. If you mouth professes financial freedom but you aren't paying off debts and building a savings as best you are able, then what faithful work are you sowing in that declaration? God is not going to change our lives in these ways when our hearts are so hard about money, time management, discipline, and relationships, that we would rather buy a new outfit and eat out than set aside ten-percent of our income for savings in addition to tithes. We would prefer to watch all manner of ratchet reality T.V. and spend hours on social media watching successful people influence others instead of reading what the Bible says about handling money, managing time and relationships, and being healthy.

At age 25 and married almost three years, I wish I had been wise enough not to skim past the books of Ecclesiastes, Proverbs, and Psalms, which are jam packed with wisdom on time management, financial freedom, and health. My husband and I have dug deep into the Bible for financial wisdom, and we found that the self-help books we were willing to spend $12-$25 on got their basic principles right from the Bible. Come on people of God, why aren't we practicing this Bible? Are we going to spend our entire lives with countless financial, relational and health issues? How many hours this year will we waste practicing envy on social media instead of surrendering to The Word and will of God, and manifesting His known will in the world to win souls for His kingdom? Why is our surrender so broken? It is because we think Christians are supposed to be poor? Let's keep it real, most of us do not READ with the intention to obey, and we do not appreciate wisdom, even though she is a tree of life (Prov 3:18).

We refuse to invest in others or ourselves in wise ways, our closets are full but savings accounts empty. We don't even have anything to give to the poor because we mismanage our funds. Proverbs 21:20 says "There is desirable treasure, and oil in the dwelling of the wise, but a foolish man squanders it." We want God to give us more power, more anointing, and take us to the nations, but we cannot even manage what little money we do have (Luke 16:11). We want God to open the windows of heaven and bless us (Mal 3:10) but we don't tithe faithfully and we do not give to others (Prov 22:8). We want God to increase our credit score but we don't even make payments on our cards, and when a payment is made, the card is used again unnecessarily. In Proverbs 22:7 NLT, the Bible says "Just as the rich rules over the poor, so the borrower is servant to the lender."

Am I advocating for believers to pursue money and networks? No way! Not Shonda! I will never encourage anyone to envy the success of unbelievers (Prov 23:17 NLT). My thesis is this: The Bible is the manual for life, including how to manage your finances, diet, schedule, and relationships. It quite clearly tells us to seek first God's kingdom (Matt 6:33) and to honor Him with what we have (Prov 3:9) because we will give an account for our decisions (Rom 14:!2). Therefore, as believers in Jesus Christ and people who claim to be living The Word of truth, we should employ every principle we can in our daily living and not allow the world to beat us at living the Bible in any area. We do not have to fall prey to covetousness every time we scroll through Instagram if we know full well that we are employing Biblical principles in our lives with the intention of having our whole lives praise God.

I continue to dwell on this topic because unfortunately, as Christians we think that we can only be broken down spiritually. Imagine the freedom of not being in debt, and the freedom of teaching your children time management, business principles, and relationship skills based on the Bible. Imagine being able to be a better example as you find increasing degrees of freedom from people and lenders as you pay your debts on time, tithe, and consistently give. Imagine giving up laziness, indiscipline, and the expectation of free handouts and becoming all that Christ wants you to be while on this earth. I dwell on this topic because we are allowing the world to define what it means for us to be successful when in fact the world gets its success principles from God's Word. Why does it not resonate with us that the abundant life Jesus came for us to have is wrapped up in ALL the Bible?

Please, do not misunderstand me beloved family. If you

do not have extra, then you do not have extra, but anybody with money for a new hairstyle, nail salon visits, concert tickets, or an expensive phone bill definitely has extra to put aside. God has called us to find fulfillment in Him, He has called us to be content with the lives we have. How can we find contentment when we are not living the Word even in our nutrition, finances, time, or work ethic? I want to be consistent, disciplined, debt free, active, and able to leave my children an inheritance to God's glory, even if that inheritance is an example of living the Word of God and excludes a wealthy fortune. I want to be able to be a continual lender and no longer a borrower, someone who can freely financially aid others, especially without causing my child to go without.

Me calling you out on your broken down surrender is not about being rich, it is not about amassing wealth and businesses but it is about not letting life just happen to you when Christ died for you to have an abundant life; He died so you can happen to life. God is concerned about your total health, otherwise money and time management would not be in the Bible. This is not a prosperity gospel chapter, this is me saying praise God with your time, money, diet, and agenda. Imagine stepping out on faith and opening the business God told you to have, and being an employer, helping others become financially independent and stable. Imagine writing that book God called you to write and it reaching 20 people or millions. Imagine starting that foundation, imagine getting that degree. Imagine being able to be an example of Christian financial stability, time management, and excellent work ethic. Imagine being able to help your parents retire early or pay off the debts of those closest to you. Imagine being able to purchase a building for your church or paying off the mortgage? Imagine being able to build a community center, or help fund international missions? How are you going to be trustworthy with those big projects when the small projects of tithing, repaying debts on time, saving, and giving cheerfully are beyond your scope of understanding? I am addressing this message to "you" but I please know that I have preached this same message to myself and in my own home first.

Beloved believers and fellow broke down Christians, the world has got us beat in this regard! We know God reigns on the just and the unjust, we know His word cannot return to Him void, and this is why unbelievers who study the Bible and enact the principles receive the blessings. They have gone on to do the impossible. They have got the mustard seed faith to move the mountain, they have matched their faith with deliberate and wise action. Meanwhile we are still busy on our knees praying, using tarrying in prayer as an excuse to run from the purposes of God that don't match our courage. If the Jesus I believe has overcome the world, and the same Spirit that raised Him from the dead, is living, actually and literally, living inside of you and I, why are we more cowardice than the world? Do you see the plan of the enemy that many of us play into? Honoring God with how you handle your time, money, networks, and health is also a way of letting your light shine before men so that they may see the God in you.

We are so much more than our prayers for God to heal us of diabetes while drinking soda every day, and so much more than our pleas with God for a financial breakthrough while using our tax returns for anything but debt repayment and savings. Beloved, we are so much more than the reflections of ourselves that we pick at in the mirror, and our frustrations over our physical appearance despite our refusal to eat healthy and exercise. We are so much more than the discontentment that creeps up inside of us as we envy the lives of others that we see on social media. Trust that you are so much more than your faithless prayers and the written goals you never push yourself to achieve. Beloved, surrender to the Word and allow yourself to be more in Jesus' name.

# A PRAYER FOR US

Oh Lord help us to surrender to Your full will for our lives. You called us to be givers so it must mean that You desire for us to have something to give. You called us to be debt free which means You intend for us to be able to obtain without borrowing. Give us a new heart Lord Jesus, one that longs to live out Your word in every area of our lives. Let us not only invite you into the "living rooms" of our lives, but also into the depths of our hidden basements. Transform our complete lives, including the way we speak, the way we handle money, the way we give to others, and the way we view Your principles. We thank You that Your word is sharper than any two-edged sword. May it divide from us laziness, procrastination, and the bliss of ignorance.

Amen.

# TUNE OUT TO TUNE IN

The Holy Spirit led my husband to take the family on a seven day fast- no meals before 6:00p.m., no social media, no television, no cell phone usage except in emergencies, and internet usage was strictly for the purpose of researching Biblical things and watching sermons. The fast was very difficult for me because I always have something going in the background as noise, because I unfortunately do not like silence. At the time I did not have a job (aside from this book), so sitting home all day watching sermons was nerve-wracking, to be honest. I know it sounds weird, but I prefer the drama of shows like The Parkers and Golden Girls for background noise. The lack of entertainment forced me to talk with God more, and to reflect on the condition of my life. Without the noise of social media or television, I could see myself better and hear His voice clearer. I believe He enjoyed our conversations.

The point here is to encourage you to break away from

media and worldly influences allowed in your home or private spaces. We live in a time when social media has become an essential part of our lives, along with television programs that are filled with perversion. Beloved, you have got to detach yourself from the negative influences of the world, from the reality TV shows, and those that promote ungodly living. You may not think it is a big deal, but you are mentally and emotionally affected by what you see on TV, why do you think there are so many commercials? Advertisers know that they can capture your emotions and money through dramatic marketing. From a spiritual perspective, TV can be a tool to distract you, overconsumption of TV leads to seeds being planted in the mind that make you choose good over godly. Listen beloved, good is not always godly and this is a lesson I learned while reflecting during this fast. I worked to be a good friend and do good things but constantly wound up with eyes shaded by the filth I observed and my ears clogged with the junk I allowed people to tell me.

So again, as believers we have got to make fasting habitual. In this era we are living in, we cannot fast from food alone, we must combine food fasting with both TV and social media fasting. Be intentional; delete the Facebook and Instagram apps so you won't tempt yourself, like I am being tempted right now. You might think I'm getting way too deep, but please recognize that the loud sounds must be turned off and the ear cleaned in order for us to hear God. Joel 2:12 tells us that fasting is a way to return to God. Since we have salvation in Jesus Christ, we know that we can stray because of the influences of the world around us and the world we allow into our homes. Both Daniel 9 and Ezra 8 also tell us that fasting is a mode of seeking God. If you're wondering why you can't hear from God at your house, then you need to fast!

Look with me at Isaiah 58:6-8 NKJV. In this scripture, God is speaking to Israel through His servant and informing them that He did not order a fast for appearance and passionless rule-following, but instead "to loose the bands of wickedness, to undo the heavy burdens, and to let the oppressed go free, and that ye break every yoke." In Matthew 9:27-29, Jesus told the disciples that a particular kind of deliverance is only by prayer and fasting. Fasting is essential; it is a means of detoxing from the world and reconnecting with the Holy Spirit, whose temple you are. Fasting is a way to be alone with God, clear the mind, and develop a keener understanding of the difference between God's voice and the enemy's. Fasting is a way to do war with the enemy and establish the unwavering faith exemplified in Isaiah 58:6-8 and Matthew 9:27-29. We fast to honor God's glory, break yokes of bondage, release burdens, clean up our lives, and bring deliverance. Beloved, do you need any of these things in your household?

Take this to heart by fasting, praying, and studying God's word. Seek His face and learn about Him by experience, so you do not have to rely on any else's testimony to keep you motivated toward God.

# A PRAYER FOR US

Father please grant us a discerning heart so we can know when we need to detox and break away from TV and social media. We know Lord, that You have not called us to live mundane and boring lives, but help us to learn to love clean and wholesome entertainment. Cause us to stop enticing ourselves to sin with the images presented on television shows and social media pages. God we want to be used by You, please help us to recognize that we have the power to shut off the voices of the world and tune in to Your voice alone. Forgive us for our lack of intentional fasting, and our over-indulgence in television. Please change our hearts, and cause us to demonstrate an even stronger love for You and greater respect for our purposes.

In Jesus' name we pray,

Amen.

# RUSTY SWORDS & DULL WEAPONRY

When I first got saved at age 13, I knew that Bible study was essential for my growth into a mature Christian. I was always a reader, and read with passion while taking notes, highlighting, underlining, and actually attempting to understand the practical and eternal value of the scriptures. My Bible looked like it had been through battle, its tattered cover barely held onto the fragile pages that were filled with notes in the margins. At that time, the Bible was my greatest ally because its words kept me engaged during the lengthy three-hour prayer meetings that I was required to attend, as my family never missed church. Eventually, the scriptures stuck and flowed naturally in my daily prayers throughout my teenage years. However, by the time I reached my sophomore year of college, I wasn't studying the Bible and praying like I used to. In fact, although I was on the leadership board for the Black gospel choir on campus, my passion for the Word of God had completely dissipated. As a result, I found myself easily ignoring the convictions and warnings of the Holy Spirit. It became easier and easier to party like a dancehall queen on the weekends, and squander my time and money without conviction. When I set goals, I found myself giving into the temptation to be undisciplined and procrastinate because I did not have God's Word about time management and purpose dwelling within me. Not reading the Word of God made it impossible for me as a Christian to fight against doing things that specifically displeased God even if they brought me a moment's pleasure.

Ephesians 6 tells us that the Word of God is the sword of the Spirit, which is a part of the whole armor of God and the only weapon in His armory. Let me take moment to say this in my own words: "The only weapon in the whole armor of God is the sword of the Spirit, which is the Word of God." The helmet of salvation, breastplate of righteousness, shield of faith, the belt of truth, and the gospel of Jesus are all used for defensive purposes, meaning they are used to protect you from deadly strikes and losing your footing. However, none of these tools are weapons. The Bible tells us that we are in spiritual warfare (Eph 6:12, 2 Corin 10:3-5, 1 Pet 5:8), so there will be times during battle that we will need to strike the enemy with a blow that cuts deep. There will also be times when we will need to take back our minds and desires. The way to accomplish this is with the Word of God.

Let's go to the specific scripture in Ephesians 6:11 AMP: "Put on the full armor of God [for His precepts are like the splendid armor of a heavily-armed soldier], so that you may be able to [successfully] stand up against all the schemes and the strategies and deceits of the devil." The amplified version of the Bible tells you what the words mean to offset confusion. In this case, we know that in order to even put on the whole armor we must know the precepts, and those precepts can be found where? In the Bible! So where am I taking you with all of this? Beloved, we are in a war and dull swords will not cut or kill. The enemy is not playing, he is an expert at being God's enemy, and the way he chooses to attack God is by getting us, God's most beloved creation, to reject fellowship with Him through sin. As such, you need to STUDY (commit to memory and enact) the word of your victorious ally, God. David asked God to teach his hands to war (Ps 144:1). You cannot commit yourself to war if you only get your word on the weekends at church and occasionally at formal Bible study.

The Bible explicitly informs us of two of its purposes: the first, that we might believe and be saved; and the second, to dissect and discern the intent of the heart. Let's check out the following scriptures:

"But these are written (recorded) in order that you may believe that Jesus is the Christ (the Anointed One), the Son of God, and that through believing and cleaving to and trusting and relying upon Him you may have life through (in) His name [through Who He is] (John 20:31 AMP)."

"For the Word that God speaks, is alive and full of power [making it active, operative, energizing, and effective]; it is sharper than any two-edged sword, penetrating to the dividing line of the [a] breath of life (soul) and [the immortal] spirit, and of joints and marrow [of the deepest parts of our nature], exposing and sifting and analyzing and judging the very thoughts and purposes of the heart (Hebrews 4:12 AMP). "

You need the Word of God not only to believe that Jesus

Christ came, but to KNOW that believing and trusting in Him means life. Furthermore, you need the word of God to be able to examine yourself! David said in Psalm 119:4-6 NLT, "You have charged us to keep your commandments carefully. Oh that my actions would consistently reflect your decrees! Then I will not be ashamed when I compare my life with your commands." The standard set for us is Jesus Christ, the Holy Spirit lives in us to guide us along the straight and narrow path that leads to eternal life.

It is critical that we also take note of David's actions in Psalm 119:4-6, he speaks about method, consistency, and accuracy. As believers we ought to *carefully* study God's Word, consistently live out God's Word so that our lives begin to mirror it, and then examine ourselves by God's Word to ensure we are looking more like Christ. Beloved, not studying the Word means we cannot even begin to discern the Holy Spirit because we don't have the written truth in our spiritual arsenal. This means that we can go to church and be misled by unbiblical doctrine and prophesies because we don't have any Word in us to measure accuracy.

The Word of God has another purpose I want to bring back to your attention for just a moment:

"All scripture is God-breathed [given by divine inspiration] and is profitable for instruction, for conviction [of sin], for correction [of error and restoration to obedience], for training in righteousness [learning how to live in conformity to God's will, both publicly and privately – behaving honorably with personal integrity and moral courage]; so that the man of God may be complete and proficient, and outfitted and thoroughly equipped for every good work (2 Timothy 3:16-17

AMP)."

Can you sense my excitement at this heavy dose of truth revealed in these two verses alone? Essentially, you can't act right, talk right, or walk right without knowing the scriptures!

Are you someone who genuinely wants to follow the example of Jesus by studying the Word but you either don't know where to start or you lack the passion to do so? Or could you be avoiding the Bible because you don't want to see yourself reflected in the scriptures, and you don't want to be told you have to change and mature? Studying the Bible to get to know God means less time for your significant other, your daily distractions, and whatever else that pulls you away from more time spent with God. We already know that the scriptures will dissect your heart; are you running from the Bible as a way to also run from revealing your truths? Here's how the enemy can trip us up: When we get saved and ask for Jesus to come into our hearts, we openly welcome His renewal of our spirits. But once renewed, we struggle to embody the new creation we become in Him because we are still running from truth found in the scriptures that will expose our hidden natures.

Beloved, God's Word is not out to harm you, rather it is there to preserve you by transforming your speech, thought process, mode of operation, and focus. God's Word is not out to harm your relationships, but to protect those people you are in relationship with from your dysfunction and vice versa. John 14:23-26 AMP tells us that loving Jesus means keeping His teachings and that the Holy Spirit (who is the Comforter, Intercessor, Advocate, and Counselor) will take that teaching to another level by revealing all things. Beloved, ask yourself a serious question: How can you even begin to reciprocate Christ's love when you don't know the teachings you should be obeying? We know the standard for reciprocating love for Christ, but can't attempt to meet it because there is no Word in us. It isn't enough to pull out your phone read the verse of the day on the Bible app and let that be the extent of your study of the Word. You have got to understand the verse, apply it to your life, pray it over your life and the lives of other believers, and meditate on it so that you can commit it to memory. Deliberately attempt to live the Word so that you can share your understanding with someone else who may be in need of the same message.

Beloved, how will you know (commit to memory, exercise, and be able to teach) His commands if you do not STUDY the Word? 2 Timothy 2:15 AMP summarizes this lesson perfectly:

"Study and be eager and do your utmost to present yourself to God approved (tested by trial), a workman who has no cause to be ashamed, correctly analyzing and accurately dividing [rightly handling and skillfully teaching] the Word of Truth."

Knowing God's Word and correctly applying it to our lives keeps us from being ashamed, partly because God protects us when we demonstrate our love for Him through obedience. This breaks down to one fundamental question: HOW DO YOU KNOW YOU LOVE JESUS? In addition, how is your love for Jesus broken? It's probably incorrect to repeat myself, but if obedience is a demonstration of love for Jesus, and you're selectively obedient, how do you know you love Jesus? Is there any proof? In writing this book, I've learned that habits create cycles. We study the Bible → apply the principles → teach the principles → use the principles against the devil to resist temptation → avoid deliberate sin → and return to studying the Bible.

Lastly, I'd like to end my thoughts on dull weaponry by touching on the inability to resist temptation when the Word is not hidden in your heart. Matthew 4:1-11 describes Jesus being tempted by the devil after fasting. The enemy caught him at a time when Jesus was weak in His body, and I don't know if Jesus was like I am, but hungry Shonda can't focus on anything else but a quick path to food. When I am hungry I struggle to be nice or even hold a conversation like a normal human being. Yet, here in Matthew 4:1-11 Jesus is being required to act like a fed person who can concentrate on right and wrong, and He resists the devil after being offered the *world*. But look at Jesus, He uses the very Word of God to combat the enticements of the enemy. Don't believe me? To overcome the enemy in the first tempting offer Jesus told Satan, "Man shall not live by bread alone, but by every word that proceeds from the mouth of God (Matt 4:4)," that can be found in Deuteronomy 8:3. Then Jesus told Satan, he was not going to tempt the Lord God, which is found in Deuteronomy 6:16. And finally, Jesus used Exodus 20:3, "You shall have no other gods but Me," to resist the last tempting offer.

If Jesus stood on the very Word of God and never sinned, how much more do we need the Word of God with all of our faults and failures? If Jesus – the Lord of Lords and King of Kings – used the Word to resist the devil, how much more do we need it when our temptations actually come from our own lustful desires (James 1:14)? Beloved, the devil is going to tempt you where you are weakest, and the Bible tells us that

God provides a way of escape. I know now that one way of escaping is through His Word, which ought to be hidden in all believers. When you have a solid understanding of the scriptures that describe your weaknesses and how giving into those weaknesses affects your relationship with God, you become equipped with the power to decisively decline the enemy's negative influences.

My brother, my sister, it has already been established that knowing the Word of God means actually applying it to our lives. To know God's Word is to know His will and conform to it. As Christians, our faith prevents us from walking blindly into an abyss of uncertainty. While there will be times when God calls us to endure something that we are unsure of, we know that whatever wringer He permits us to endure it is for our eternal benefit (Rom 5:3-5). You don't have to wonder about who you are and where you fit in because studying and knowing God's Word reveal your true self and prevent you from suffering an identity crisis as so many believers do. In James 1:23-24 AMP the Bible says that if you are a hearer of the Word but not a doer, you will have an identity crisis:

"For if anyone only listens to the Word without obeying it and being a doer of it, he is like a man who looks carefully at his [own] natural face in a mirror; For he thoughtfully observes himself, and then goes off and promptly forgets what he was like."

I used to wonder why I acted so much like a chameleon – I could be a Christian among Christians, but a compromiser among non-believers. It was because I wasn't studying God's Word and did not know what I was supposed to be doing, therefore I did not know who I was. As I said previously, this walk through our life journey is cyclic, just like the seasons and the cycles of life. When God's Word is not in you, you find yourself backsliding and troubled over why you can't seem to get life in rightful order, and why your desire to live for God doesn't match your actions. You find yourself acting like you aren't a chosen generation, the redeemed of the Lord, a royal priesthood, and sanctified to show God's virtues here on the earth (1 Peter 2:9). I am speaking not just from the Word, but telling you that I have experienced this very thing. In college, I attended church every Sunday but never truly studied the Word for myself and continued to act a fool because I had no compass to guide me. This is evidence that you can be heavily churched, but minimally changed. Loving Jesus is demonstrated through honoring His teachings and knowing who you are. Your love and faith in Jesus is proven daily in your private life, and not solely within the safety of the church.

Family, let us mature together. Jesus hung with sinners, but He never acted ungodly because He was the Word. We live in a time where mass media encourages alignment with the universe and not God, so as Christians we need the Word so we can mirror Christ and not this new ageism that is on the rise. When we know the Word of God, we are able to stand firm by the power of the Holy Spirit. God's Word will transform our thinking and help us recognize and escape the traps of the enemy. The Word of God stored up inside of us allows us to be influencers for God's glory instead of being influenced to our own detriment. As Christians we don't get to loosely throw around the phrase "God ain't through with me yet" as an excuse for our behavior. The fact of the matter is; God isn't through with anyone until His Kingdom comes. Make yourself so busy with fulfilling the kingdom's business that you get out of your own way and the way of others' by living the word of truth.

## A PRAYER FOR US

Oh God who is our home from time immemorial, we need a renewed passion for Your Word. We don't study like we should, nor do we read to be refined, perfected and matured. Your word Oh God is profitable for correction, but we struggle with the spirit of offense because we don't know that correction is for those You love, so we take everything inappropriately personal. We want to overcome these identity crises so we can help others, we want to be able to cut the enemy and his schemes with Your Word like Jesus did. Oh God, restore to us the joy of Your salvation and the joy of knowing Your word so that we may live it out and be a bright light in our communities.

Amen.

LASHONDA JEAN-JACQUES

# 4

# BROKE DOWN PURSUIT

# THE ROUGH SIDE OF THE MOUNTAIN

One of the things I really struggled with on this Christian journey was my motivation to keep moving forward in God's will. I would get so energized by the revival and be fully convinced that I could press on living for the Lord but after a few bad decisions or a beat down from life, I would find myself discouraged. I pondered if being a Christian was too hard for me, after all, life was throwing me hard blows and I could not see if God was not *making haste* to help me. Let's examine Exodus 6:9 KJV, "So Moses told the people of Israel what the Lord had said, but they refused to listen anymore. They had become too discouraged by the brutality of their slavery." A truth we fail to acknowledge is that Exodus 6:9 becomes reality for us when life gets hard and issues threaten to rob us of rejuvenation and progress. A lack of motivation inspires rebellion, a rebellion that is rash and careless like the Israelites'. By Exodus 16:3, the Israelites were complaining that they should have stayed in Egypt where they would have more than just manna to eat, despite their enslavement. Later on in Numbers 14:4, the Israelites threatened to elect a new leader and return to Egypt. Discouragement is just that dangerous, it makes us long for Egypt and causes us to remember things the way they were not. We get tired of waiting and decide to either return to the old Egypt or look for a new one by which to be enslaved.

During Bible study on Exodus and Numbers I thought to myself, "How in the world are the Israelites going to get back across the Red Sea?" Beloved, you cannot expect God to part the Red Sea for you to run back to Egypt and serve foreign gods as a slave when He has planned for you to live freely, serving The One true living God in a land flowing with "milk and honey." I think about what a taste of milk and honey must be for us on this side of heaven, surely it is not limited to material riches and the approval of man. I imagine milk and honey must taste as sweet as John 14:27 NKJV sounds, "Peace I leave with you, My peace I give to you; not as the world gives do I give to you. Let not your heart be troubled, neither let it be afraid." Or perhaps it feels sturdy like John 16:33 NLT, "In this world you will have trouble. But take heart! I have overcome the world." Maybe it feels like the entire Psalm 23, and feels as patient as Ps 62:1-2 NKJV "I wait quietly before God, for my victory comes from Him. He alone is my rock and my salvation, my fortress where I will never be shaken." Or suppose that milk and honey feels as beautiful as Psalm 63:2-5 NLT:

"I have seen you in the sanctuary and gazed upon your power

and glory. Your unfailing love is better than life itself; how I praise you! I will praise You as long as I live, lifting up my hands to you in prayer. Your satisfy me more than the richest feast. I will praise you with songs of joy."

The way I see it, all Broke Down Christians have the same choices: to die by the Red Sea hoping God will support their return to slavery, to remain stagnant and die in the wilderness, or keep moving toward the Promised Land. My brother, my sister, we truly do have a promised land, if not then Jesus would not have revealed that He went to prepare a place for us in John 14:3. There will be many wildernesses to endure and many seas to cross by faith, so you can't stop at this one beloved, you cannot quit and turn your heart back to Egypt this time around. Every time we begin to resent where God has us, we turn our hearts back to Egypt. You can choose to always be in the spiritually, emotionally, physically and mentally dilapidated condition that you are in right now, or you can choose to keep walking toward the truth. Keep walking toward the very truth that you were predestined for a great work (Rom 8:29), that produces fruit in this life and bountiful fruit in eternity (John 15:16). Keep walking knowing that there is a reward for finishing this race with your passion for Jesus still intact and your heart full of the love that you have shared with others along your journey.

Beloved, discouragement is the place you end up when you perceive that you are empty. When I was in labor with my son, I had 14 hours of mild pains that were very tolerable and didn't hinder me from operating as usual. But in the 15th hour, the last hour before I would begin to push, it felt like my world had turned upside down. I was no longer able to mentally cope with the pain and I began to beg for an epidural. However, God had another plan. By the 16th hour, I was on the brink of promise with no epidural, completely exhausted from pain, and had stopped pushing to scream out, "I don't have any more to give, I don't." My husband demanded that I submit to this calling of motherhood and push our baby boy's head out. My midwife kept telling me I could go beyond that point, she told me to push until the pain was greatest, until it burned hottest and then keep going even further.

Can you see the analogy in this experience? In life you may get to a point where you perceive that you don't have any more of yourself to give. You grow tired of pushing on and pressing forward, tired of the cycle of backsliding after a good run and having others witness your downfall. You have so much more to give on this journey. I know you are exhausted and discouraged, but you cannot stop moving forward. I am fully convinced that you are not empty, you can make it to the point of pain where it burns beyond belief and your mind is filled with doubts that you'll ever see God's promise for your life come to pass, but you can push through and still keep going. Don't turn away from Christ's calling because you are tired of giving but never receiving, tired of being kind to mean people, and tired of working hard to forgive but always having your past thrown in your face. Don't you dare run back to Egypt!

Discouragement is a natural part of life, just like sadness. Much like prolonged discouragement, prolonged sadness becomes the disease of depression, and it is for this reason that Egypt will entice you to return back to a familiar past. Don't you dare allow the peace of obedience to be disrupted! The peace is yours to have, and Christ has given it to you for this very moment when life in Christ seems to be at its hardest. Beloved, that peace is yours so that you may be courageous and confident through it all, confident that the suffering is not in vain and confident that God is greater than your feelings and your past; confident that He will re-purpose every pain for His glory and your reward. Know that even though you cannot hang out with everyone or go to every event, your obedience to God and your continued progression will win for you a prize far greater than the slavery of Egypt or the pain of the wilderness. Beloved family, commit to memory John 16:33 AMP:

"I have told you these things, so that in Me you may have [perfect] peace and confidence. In the world you have tribulation and trials and distress and frustration; but be of good cheer [take courage; be confident, certain, undaunted]! For I have overcome the world. [I have deprived it of power to harm you and have conquered it for you.]"

No matter how life is going, the broken down Christian in you will want to find fault, it will want to beat you up and tell you what you should have and could have done if you went any other way but the way the Holy Spirit was leading you. Be encouraged about going in God's direction, if for no other reason than the fact that on God's path, your life echoes beautifully in eternity. As a living sacrifice to God, the aroma you give off is beautiful and pure in His nostrils. Don't turn back to Egypt!

## A PRAYER FOR YOU

My great God, Father and Deliverer, thank You for my brother and sisters reading this, for they are not beyond You, and their hurt is not beyond Your heart. You feel with them, and You understand the heart and discouragement they feel when people use them, malign their character, or reject them. You understand how it feels to be marked by the pains of regret. You understand what it feels like to be hurt by life, as You had to destroy the whole world, physically abandon Your own people, and destroy Your own son just to win us back. LORD GOD, help my brothers and sisters to remember Your promises when they are struggling to overcome. May they run to Your word and not back to Egypt, may they turn their ears to sermons and The Bible instead of to Satan's lies. Cause them to set their eyes, heart, minds and lips on eternity with You rather than on all the "shoulda, coulda, wouldas" of life. Great God, cause them to be filled with Your joy when they retreat to the throne room, cause them to take back the peace they surrendered and give them the wisdom to utilize it in the time of discouragement. Oh God, I come to You in Jesus Name, praying, please don't let any of us run back to Egypt.

Amen.

## TOO MUCH WAIT

    To those of you who are still waiting for sunny weather to come before you step foot outside, STOP WAITING! You will never leave the house! If you are waiting for conditions to be perfect to start that business God told you to start, then you will never own it. When I began writing this book, I intentionally took breaks to allow life to happen to me because I felt so unqualified to give advice on Christianity. In my mind, I was a mess that was not the least bit qualified to deliver this message. I told myself that I needed to wait until I was "perfect" so I could then reveal to others how to also claim that perfection in their lives. God granted me a proverbial slap in the face, because God didn't ask me about the condition of my life or if I had any achievements to announce on Facebook. Instead, He told me to write this book. He didn't ask me if I was qualified – He qualified me when He gave me this assignment. Because of this, it reaffirmed to me that waiting for the rain to stop and the sun to shine before going outside was a detrimental mindset. Thankfully, I learned this lesson from the Israelites and not the hard way entirely on my own. I ask that you walk with me to Numbers 13:31-33 AMP:

But the men who had gone up with him said, 'We are not able to go up against the people, for they are stronger than we.' And they gave the children of Israel a bad report of the land which they had spied out, saying, 'The land through which we have gone as spies is a land that devours its inhabitants, and all the people whom we saw in it are men of great stature. There we saw the giants (the descendants of Anak came from the giants); and we were like grasshoppers in our own sight, and so we were in their sight.'"

In this scripture, the 10 men decided that it was not the right time to pursue the promise of God because Canaan was filled with giants. The people were so paranoid by the report of the men they decided they would choose another leader and return to Egypt (Numbers 14:4). On the other hand, in Numbers 14:6-9:

Joshua and Caleb reported, "the land we have passed through and explored is exceedingly good. If the LORD is pleased with us, He will lead us into that land... and will give it to us. Only do not rebel against the LORD and do not be afraid of the people of the land..."

So just as there was a tug-of-war among the Israelites in the wilderness, recognize that you too are in the crossroads of the wilderness and the promised land, and the only choice to be made is to return to Egypt or press forward toward the promise in faith. When you choose to wait, you demonstrate your willingness to forfeit your promise and that your heart has turned back to Egypt (Acts 7:39). Choosing to wait also means that those who were to accompany you have their motivation, courage, and drive to move forward stifled or killed. We know what happened to the Israelites; only two of those who stood in that crowd cowering to go back to Egypt made it to the promise land, and it was the two who dared to believe God and speak up for His plans.

Numbers 13 and 14 beg the question, "What are you seeing when you look out into the space between you and the promise?" While Ammiel and the other nine saw the giants and the terror of impending war, Joshua and Caleb saw God's description of a land that was good and ripe for the conquering, along with God's promise to their father Abraham. Beloved, the obstacles you see when you look out into the world is partly the reason why you wrap yourself in the comfort of waiting. When writing this book, I tried to focus on God's desire to reach you and me. If this was God's test of obedience, I wanted to pass with flying colors. The point is, you need to look at the obstacle you are waiting to tackle the way God looks at it. You need to recognize that there are people waiting for you to help meet their mentoring, networking, spiritual, emotional, or financial needs. There are people waiting on your example of faithfulness and integrity. Do not look out and be intimidated by the giants, oppressors, and the devouring landscape; look out and witness Jesus on the water welcoming you with open hands and giving you permission to walk on it too. Look beyond the darkness and see the purpose of your journey. When you got saved, you were asking what Peter asked on the sea of Galilee in Matthew

14:28 NKJV: "Lord, if it is You, command me to come to You on the water." Jesus has commanded us to go out into the rain, into the bad conditions, and into the drought to do the seemingly impossible, regardless of our qualifications.

Beloved, waiting is the equivalent of hiding your light and refusing to take it wherever light is needed, and therefore hindering someone's relief. I remember when I was stuck on the concept of waiting, it caused me to endure so much more hardship than necessary. Consequently, I had to overcome even more of myself, because in refusing to obey immediately, I was building up pride. Waiting is the equivalent of telling yourself "God does not know eternity because clearly this is not the right time." When I finally got myself in the right mental state of mind to write this book, my computer crashed and the book was not backed up on a hard drive. Then, when I was finally able to retrieve some of the book, I put it on my to-do list to complete during my maternity leave, but went into labor the day after writing that list. Because of my delayed obedience, I spent many late nights struggling to nurse my son and type at the same time. If you've been a first time mom living away from your family, you understand the sheer torture of exhaustion and worry that you endure while trying to both recover from giving birth and nurture a helpless little human being. Beloved, please don't be like me. Don't wait for more free time, learn to manage the time you have right now and honor God every step of the way. You don't have all the money together? Okay. Use your imagination and innovate. Don't wait for the feelings of inadequacy to pass, build your courage with action. Stop wondering if it's your perfect season to move and get on top of your assignment.

You want to know the right time to do God's will? Right

when He tells you to "GO." Do not walk behind God's will, walk in stride with it by the power of the Holy Spirit. Do not deny yourself the chance to taste and see that He is good on another level; do not deny others the chance to encounter Him in you. If you are waiting, ask yourself one pivotal question, "What answer will I give Jesus for this delay?" Delayed obedience is still disobedience, and I know this from experience. Let us repent and walk in faith. You waiting is not in faith, the faith you say you have is proven when you go as He told you, when He told you. You delay because you are waiting for your courage to catch up with you, but there is no courage coming. Christ is our personal courage – lean on Him and take the jump, despite the giants. In my case, it did not matter that there seemed to be so many others also writing Christian books. God called me to write this book for a specific reason, even if it is just for one soul. Even if that one soul is me.

Dear fellow broken down Christian, the time to go outside is NOW, because we only have RIGHT NOW! Not only is tomorrow not promised, but your assumption that tomorrow is guaranteed is prideful and spiritually unhealthy. No, you don't have accomplish everything on your goals list today, but you do need to be intentional about making considerable strides toward beginning and completing what God has called you to do. Yes, parts of you are broken, and life often invites you to have a pity party for yourself, but keep in mind that your healing is wrapped up in obedience to whatever call God has placed on your life. Do not be so consumed by your issues and daily schedule that you don't have time to pour out yourself in loving service to Christ by serving others. RIGHT NOW is the time to move out of disobedience and forfeiture into obedience, purpose, and promise. Mark 6:7-9 NLT explains this concept perfectly:

"And He called His twelve disciples together and began sending them out two by two, giving them authority to cast out evil spirits. He told them to take nothing for their journey except a walking stick—no food, no traveler's bag, no money. He allowed them to wear sandals but not to take a change of clothes."

Jesus required His disciples to be "ill-equipped" in the eyes of the world, and they were told not to travel with even basic necessities, let alone luxuries. Can you imagine being sent to travel a foreign country with no money and no luggage? The disciples were not Bible scholars like the Pharisees and Sadducees, in fact, scripture shows that they had to keep asking Jesus what the parables meant. They continuously struggled in their faith BUT their calling was discipleship and they followed their God-given assignment to go, preach, and set others free on His authority alone.

Each of us has a purpose. God has predestined us to do good works in one or many capacities, but too many of us are looking for qualifications that the world will recognize as success. Actively following Jesus was the training ground for the disciples and He equipped them with what they needed to cast out demons. They had no degrees in hand to put on their resumes; before following their calling, they held menial jobs as tax collectors and fishermen. In the eyes of the world, they were unqualified to cast out anything but nets and fees. It was the authority of Christ that qualified them back then, just as He does for you and I today. From my personal experience, Jesus still operates this way with believers, challenging us to see ourselves as ill-equipped or fully able through Him. Today, He still requires us to go out without having all the money, or the right networks and contacts. He sends us out with a two-fold assignment – to serve and to trust that God is actively Jehovah Jireh. Actively following the leading of the Holy Spirit is what qualifies us. Christ's authority qualifies us to fulfill our purposes, so there is no need to wait until the storm passes before we decide to step out on faith. Because of obedience, the disciples moved from discipleship to apostleship, and from novice followers to teachers and leaders.

Beloved, demonstrate your faith by doing the impossible (James 2:18: "I will show you my faith, by my deed") and do not wait for the perfect conditions to do so because you will never accomplish anything that way (Ecc 11:4). Indiscipline kills (Prov 5:23), but more importantly, if you are aware of your purpose and refuse to fulfill it, it is a sin (James 4:17). John the Baptist tells us that we have to "do the work while it is day for the night is coming." The "night" that is coming is death. If your death unexpectedly comes tomorrow, what will your life have meant? When you die, will your loved ones be able to celebrate that you lived a life of purpose by serving others with your passions and skills? Or will the good deeds they speak about come few and far between?

Doing what God asks of us has this beautiful way of filling us up, not just because it proves we can be disciplined and faithful, but because it allows us to contribute to someone else's understanding of Jesus Christ through the nature of our service. We help the world to see that Christianity does not mean that we are slaves to an organized religion, but that we are choosing the greatest purpose and opportunity to serve of all.

## A PRAYER FOR US

Most kind and awesome Heavenly Father, I come before You on behalf of my myself, and my brothers and sisters who struggle to live by faith. LORD we know that anything not done in faith is sin and it displeases You, so please cause us to see every faithless act in this way. Forgive our delayed obedience, You spoke to us and we arrogantly disobeyed, concocting excuses in our own minds as to why not trusting You was the right thing to do. LORD please renew our minds as we study Your Word and prevent us from focusing on the giants and oppressors. Allow us to place our only focus on You.

Even now Father, as I have taken my step out, I pray that You would cause my brother and sister to take their own steps to move out of disobedience and forfeiture into obedience and promise. In the name of Jesus, urge them by the Holy Spirit to move, before it is too late. For they can do ALL things through Jesus Christ who strengthens them, including obey You and honor His sacrifice by living for Your glory. In Jesus' Name, I pray,

Amen.

## JOURNAL ENTRY: PROCRASTINATION

*Some of us Christians may already know our purposes or have been given assignments, and we are just slunkin' (slacking). But we all know that slunkin' is not okay. In August 2015, I had completed the major content for this book, and only had to re-read and make some edits before sending it off to the editor. I intentionally went from being productive for Jesus to being too busy to complete it. Note that procrastination doesn't only mean lollygagging, but also means putting off the most urgent task for another. This book was an urgent assignment from The Lord and I put it off for school and work, fully aware that I could have accomplished all of these tasks simultaneously. As I was in prayer one night, it hit me that procrastination is one of the most selfish things I can do. There is someone who is in great need of the message I have to offer, and I decided within myself to be too busy to give him or her my help. When I procrastinate, it places someone else's faith on the line.*

*I immediately repented.*

*Beloved LaShonda, it is not right to procrastinate, your purpose is not solely about you.*

## A PRAYER FOR US

Lord Jesus, "teach us to realize the brevity of life that we may grow in wisdom" (Ps 90:12), and "remind us that our days are numbered (Ps 39:4 NLT). Give us a brand new heart to obey You, so that we may honor You with these talents, skills, and passions bestowed upon us. Give us an undivided heart (Ps 86:12) so that we can be faithful in fulfilling Your purpose. Forgive our procrastination, for we know it is prideful and therefore sinful. Lord we surrender our laziness, our fear, and our indiscipline to You. We do not want to die with our potential buried inside of us, we want to invest the seeds of love, hope, purpose and forgiveness in others so that they might be changed by Your power and love. Please give us new fire, new direction, and new conviction to run the race to completion. Give us the courage to do the impossible; we know You have already given us the power. Lord Jesus, please grant us accountability partners who will drag out of us the courage we refuse to have. We want to be responsible and responsive, we want to prove faithful and dependable to Your honor and glory. In Your name we do pray,

Amen.

# 5

# BROKE DOWN CONVICTION

Matt 26:37-38 *"... And He began to be sorrowful and troubled. Then He said to them, 'My soul is overwhelmed to the point of death...'"*

I believe the reality of His separation from God was what brought Jesus to such immense sorrow that He felt a heavy heart alone would kill Him. The way He would die, cursed on a tree (Gal 3:13; Deut 21:23), for seemingly hopeless people. Some of us live on a fence and risk separation from God. While we may speak about Him or attend church, some of us live godless lives because we don't actually believe He has any power or cares about us. Unfortunately, we are not as troubled as we should be about this. Truly, it should bother us to not be living in God's will. It should bother us to see another person continually digging pits for themselves, be they financial, spiritual, emotional, or otherwise. It should bother us when people die having never acknowledged Jesus. It should drive us to deep prayer when we see each other living compromising lifestyles.

"In the last days, the love of many will wax cold (Matthew 24:12)."

# ONLY GOD CAN JUDGE ME

"Only God can judge me," is statement that has been the defense of many for why no one should call them out for certain behavior(s). Jesus is explicit about this in Luke 6: 37 & 41-43 AMP:

"Do not judge, and you will not be judged. Do not condemn and you will not be condemned. Why do you look at the speck that is in your brother's eye, but do not notice *or* consider the log that is in your own eye? How can you say to your brother, 'Brother, allow me to take out the speck that is in your eye,' when you yourself do not see the log that is in your own eye? You hypocrite (play actor, pretender), first take the log out of your own eye, and then you will see clearly to take out the speck that is in your brother's eye. For there is no good tree which produces bad fruit, nor, on the other hand, a bad tree which produces good fruit."

To judge means to pass sentence or punish. Let's get

one thing straight – being honest with someone about their self-destructive behavior and the results it can yield is not judging. On the other hand, telling someone "You are going to hell" (which is not the same as "You are on a path that leads to hell") is passing judgment and condemning. Only Jesus can tell someone where he or she will spend eternity. I am deeply disturbed by believers calling everything judgment, when the word, spoken by Jesus Himself is very clear: your fruit is your ID card. If you continue to produce spiritually unhealthy things, you have judged yourself by your choices. However, according to Jude 1:23, when another believer sees you engaging in ungodly behavior, it is their job to correct or warn you. It is essential that the believer who is attempting to correct you is not also struggling with the same issues. For example, if you are struggling with an addiction to pornography and you find me (a fellow Christian) also watching porn, then you would be a hypocrite to correct me because we are planting the same kinds of seeds. Likewise, if you are a gossiper telling me to stop gossiping, you have no place to correct me because you have yet to rise above your own flaw. However, if you have overcome your struggles, you can help another overcome the same issue.

Saying to someone, "This isn't what God wants for your life," or more bluntly, "You need to stop sleeping around" is not judging. Saying something is wrong that the Bible explicitly says is wrong is not a judgment, it is a statement that declares "I recognize that fruit on your tree." The fruit you bear shows your heart. I only have the right to call you out on your wrong as I see it if I am not committing the same fault. If I am indulging in the same wrong as you, then my sight is not clear and I therefore do not have the spiritual clarity to see help you see your problem's root or solution. Please do not misconstrue my point here – there are definitely Christians who genuinely love to sentence and punish people who offend God's law without acknowledging that they themselves are offenders too. However, this is not about them, this is about believers who need to be told that they are headed down a path of self-destruction using, "Only God can judge me" to thwart correction. It is better for us to hold each other accountable, and better for you to examine yourself now, than for you to get to the end of your life to hear Jesus say "Depart from Me, I never knew you (Matt 7:21-23)." When people call you out on your laziness, your procrastination, your sexual sin, your habitual lying, or your nasty attitude, they should not do so for the purpose of embarrassing you publicly, but instead as a means to help steer you down the right path.

I often find such comedy in the irony of human behavior. We are open to correction in some forms, but not others. We are ok with reading self-help books that basically beat us across the head for making stupid decisions, and then advise us on how to make good ones. However, when it comes to taking advice about our soul's salvation and walk with Christ, we take offense when someone offers constructive criticism. As your sister in Christ, it would be wrongful of me to watch you self-destruct and not attempt to help you through your struggle. Doing so would be like a doctor knowing about the dangers of STDs and not advising his patients to use protection. I have even seen believers pacify the truth by saying "I am not God, so I cannot judge." How is speaking the truth (out of love) judging? If no one ever corrected you, how would you know that you were wrong? If no one pointed out the holes in your pocket, how would you know that you were losing your money?

Beloved, hear me with your heart and your mind. If no one in your circle requires you to strive for excellence and uphold your values as a Christian, then you are in the wrong crowd. If you are recognized by your fruit and you bear bad apples, then you cannot be offended when someone brings your rotten apples to your attention. This is no time for "lotion, petting, and powdering" as my mom would say, this is a time for maturity! Grow up! It is better for all of us to correct our behaviors right now with the help of the Holy Spirit, than get to judgement day and have to answer to Jesus for refusing to change. Ask the Holy Spirit for discernment so that you can know the difference between judgment and correction, and so you can also discern a friend from a foe. Never separate yourself from honest people, those who are not afraid to tell you when you stink and show you how to maintain good hygiene (metaphorically speaking).

When I was a baby Christian, I would cry every time I got corrected because my pastor "ene (ain't) had no shame" (as we say in the Bahamas). She always told us that our blood would not be on her hands and made it a point to correct us whenever we did wrong. She would not give us the opportunity to say we were not warned about our behavior. Her intention was the perfect reason for me to stop crying about getting corrected and start rejoicing that someone cared enough about my eternity to say "Shonda, this is wrong for you, it is going to lead to..." I am thankful for people who mean me well and correct me, especially those who have worn the same shoes and can encourage me by their testimony.

My brother, my sister – the fruit you bear is in accordance with the choices you have made. The fruit on these trees feed people, and the closer someone is to us, the more fruit they consume from your life. Souls are waiting on you to produce the fruit of the Spirit so that you can feed them. So will you take offense when it is brought to your attention that you are bearing rotten fruit, or will you choose to grow and improve? Constructive criticism, correction, or whatever you want to call it, is only proof that people can recognize the types of choices you have made. A sister or brother in Christ acknowledging your actions and challenging you to do better should not be taken as judgment. Do not take offense to statements like:

- "Fornication is a sin. Save yourself for marriage because that is what pleases God."
- "You don't need to dress so revealing, your body is God's temple, and sexy clothing might compromise the message of salvation. You can be fabulous and covered too."
- Or more sternly, "I thought you were saved, why are you going to the club and listening to this hypersexual music? You don't need to compromise the message of Jesus Christ that you carry by indulging in these things."

    This chapter is not meant to embarrass anyone, but rather to put an end to the misuse of "Only God can judge me" as an excuse for poor behavior. Be thankful when you encounter someone that will look out for your soul. In the world we live in today, we have more people encouraging compromise than encouraging holiness. Your sins are between you and God, and no believer has the right to hold them against you. However, every believer has a right to expect you to be who you say you are, and that believer has an obligation to cover your sins with love. This same love corrects and does not encourage continuation in sin (Prov 3:12). Correction comes from fact not opinion, and those facts are found in the Bible.

For example, "Thou shalt not commit adultery" is a clear command written in Exodus 20:14, so being corrected about your adulterous ways is not someone's opinion, it is God's word! Learn the difference!

Another scripture we can examine is Jude 1:22-23 which says: "Be merciful to those who doubt; save others by snatching them from the fire, to others show mercy, mixed with fear – hating even the clothing stained by corrupted flesh." There you have it beloved! Right there in the very Word of God it tells believers to SNATCH each other from the fire. Imagine a mother snatching up her child for misbehaving; our responsibilities to each other are similar. We are not to watch one another walk towards destruction and not speak up in love as we are led by the Holy Spirit. You are responsible to God to warn another believer.

Hebrews 10:24-25 AMP says:

"And let us consider and give attentive, continuous care to watching over one another, studying how we may stir up (stimulate and incite) to love and helpful deeds and noble activities; Not forsaking or neglecting to assemble together [as believers', as] ...admonishing, warning, urging and encouraging one another, and all the more faithfully as you see the day approaching."

Beloved, we are in the last days and we know that many will be deceived and fall away from Christ (1 Tim 4:1). We have no time to walk in offense when others are "warning, urging, and encouraging" us with the truth of our clearly destructive ways. What is the point of being offended by a Christian brother or sister supposedly "judging" you when God knows the very deepest of secrets in your life? Do you not believe heaven will rejoice at your growth and maturity, and that God will be pleased that you took advantage of an honest moment for His glory and your eternal reward? Hebrews 10:24-25 clearly tells us to get under each other's rugs and expose the pile of dirt conveniently swept underneath. Let me repeat – no one has the right to hold your sins against you, and no one should publicly shame you for sinning. At the same time, trust that those who try to help have been led by the Holy Spirit. While at times, the delivery of those corrections from others may be off-putting to you., it is essential not to get wrapped up in the delivery. Instead to get wrapped up in the message and then go unwrap yourself before God in prayer and fasting.

No matter the approach, always be thankful when someone submits to the Holy Spirit and comes to warn, encourage, and snatch you from the fire. I am sure that if the future you could look through time, he or she would be shouting at you to be grateful and change your current ways. Why regret later on, the correction you can heed today?

Let every Christian man and woman examine themselves!

# THE PROPHET, THE PROPHELIAR, & YOU

Prophecy in the Christian church has gotten such a bad reputation in the eyes of the world, and of course it is primarily due to false prophets and the misuse of the office of prophecy to gain wealth. However, what adds to the degrading reputation of prophetic ministry in general is the fact that too many Christians can be found church-hopping in constant search of a new Word. Unfortunately, many of us believers still thrive on emotional hype; we only get into the worship if the musicians excite us enough and we only get into the preached Word if the pastor is whooping and hollering. When guest prophets come into town, many believers flock to the church without even praying for discernment looking for a Word from God. The packed pews never bothered me, I thought, "wow, all of these people are here to experience God in ways they haven't on their own?" That was until a family member got defrauded of tens of thousands of dollars by a guest prophet. After that, it began to break my heart to see believers who would barely attend Bible study, give offering, or participate in ministry at their own church, suddenly come up with $1000 so they could "hear from God," at someone else's church.

Beloved, don't get me wrong, I fully believe in the gift of prophecy and the anointing to prophesy. I know full well that the Holy Spirit can speak through whomever He pleases, whenever He pleases. However, I have to wonder what makes us itch so bad for a Word from God through a prophet about a house or car when we know full well we have no prayer life, no worship life, and aren't faithful tithers. As a Christian, not being a faithful tither means you will have cursed pockets. Despite knowing this, many believers are still running from church to church to catch the visiting prophet or prophetess for a word about a financial breakthrough. Even with God 1+ 1 =2, if you think I am joking, turn your Bibles to Luke 16:10 NLT, "If you are faithful in little things, you will be faithful in large ones. But if you are dishonest in little things, you won't be honest in greater responsibilities."

The problem with being a prophecy chaser is not with the prophets, but with you. When the many prophecies you have collected over the years have not come to fruition in the time frame you see fit, you not only begin to pronounce the prophet as fraudulent, but you begin to resent the very gift and office of prophecy. When you chase prophecy after prophecy, you make yourself vulnerable to dishonoring such a powerful gift from God. As a result, when you are given a Word that you did not solicit, you refuse to receive or believe it. Prophecy is essential to the development of the Christian and the Church. In 1 Corinthians 14:4, Apostle Paul told the church of Corinth that the gift of prophecy because it edifies the church.

Let's be honest here – the Bible tells us "Beloved, do not believe every spirit [speaking through a self-proclaimed prophet]; instead test the spirits to see whether they are from God, because many false prophets *and* teachers have gone out into the world (1 John 4:1 AMP)." Being a prophecy chaser makes us too emotional, and anything controlled by emotions breeds regret. When you're too emotional, you don't listen carefully and you do not test the spirits as the Bible admonishes. The Bible tells us in 1 John 4:1 that false prophets and teachers are among us, and the way they get us hooked to their teaching is through our own blinding emotions. Rather than direct our anger inwards, we get mad at God because a word (a word that was never His) didn't come to pass.

Beloved, you have got to seek God for yourself and not chase prophets. God will not send you a blessing (whether that be a promotion or anything else you desire) when you are not in the right state to receive it. Constant complaints, ungratefulness, and consistent laziness do not lay the foundation for you to receive a word about increase in material blessings. If you want to hear from God, GO FAST AND PRAY! I can tell you from experience that if you seek God with your whole heart, He will indeed make Himself known to you.

In 2013 when I was 22 and living on my Grandma's couch, I was in a serious bout of despair over the fact that I wasn't going to graduate school in the Fall of that year. I needed a Word from God, and that night, I prayed the longest prayer I had ever prayed in my life. I was so determined to find God that every time I got tired, I found myself saying, "God, I'm not going to stop praying until You speak to me. I need You to come on this couch and please speak to me." Five hours into praying, the Lord spoke to me very clearly and told me He wanted me to write this book, to write about being a broken Christian and reviving my passion for Christ – that was what He wanted me to do.

After moving away from my Grandma's house a few months later, I spent a lot of my time studying the Bible and writing prayers, but never told anyone about my assignment from God. Over time, I began to get discouraged. One day, I opened my Facebook inbox to see a message from a mentor, and she told me that God said to keep writing. Beloved, that fired me right back up of course! My point in recounting this experience was to show you that God will answer you, it may not be what you want to hear but He will always answer you. The night that after God spoke to me about this book, He told me, "Now go to sleep," and it was the most peaceful sleep I had since 2009.

Beloved, God's love truly desires to see us prosper and that includes being encouraged, corrected and instructed to help us grow spiritually. This is illustrated in 1 Corinthians 14:3 AMP:

"But [on the other hand] the one who prophesies speaks to people for edification [to promote their spiritual growth] and [speaks words of] encouragement [to uphold and advise them concerning the matters of God] and [speaks words of] consolation [to compassionately comfort them]."

You cannot run around expecting every prophecy to answer your prayers for a promotion, a house, or a car when you know that you can't make it through the work day without grumbling and complaining about your boss, you don't handle your finances well, and the apartment you do have is always unkempt. You cannot expect to receive only the encouraging prophecies and not the edifying ones, and you just cannot constantly have an itch to run around from church to church looking for a Word.

Beloved, chase God, not prophets. If you attend a prophetic ministry, you will be sure to encounter a personal Word from God in that forum. However, if you don't and God wants to get a Word to you, know that HE IS GOD...HE DOESN'T NEED YOUR HELP TO SPEAK TO YOU. Your instinct should not be to run to a prophet for an answer to your prayers, your instinct should be to run to turn your plate down in fasting and get in your prayer closet.

How many more pastors, preachers, evangelists, deacons, priests, and other church leaders have to be caught in scandals or arrested for domestic violence for you and I to realize one key thing? KNOW GOD FOR YOURSELF! Know where to find Him, and then dwell with Him to learn His voice. How many church leaders have come in the name of Jesus and deceived weak sheep, making them pay for *a prophetic Word*? Always retreating to the comfort of a human representative of God means you might actually get human opinion and not God's Word. Let me pause to remind you that this is not about the gift of prophecy, the office of the prophet, or about your own prophet, pastor, bishop or neighbor – it is about you and your heart toward prophecy. Growing up in a very small church with less than 100 members, my Pastor taught us that you should not get emotional about a prophetic Word, you should get prayerful. Even when she was the one delivering the prophetic message, she encouraged us to pray for discernment. She advised us to this not out of doubt about her calling as a prophet of Jesus Christ, but out of wisdom.

At this point you might be thinking, "Shonda, I have been struggling and I just need an on time Word from the Lord." Beloved, God knows better than we do what we need, how much we can handle, and when we can handle the dosage He will release. He did not call any of us to spend more time chasing down a prophet than we do seeking Him. He did not call us to try and purchase a Word from Him, but to spend time with Him doing His will. Dig into His Word and recognize that He gave you an eternal Word and lifetime promises that you can be busy calling to His attention through prayer. Take comfort in knowing that His Word will guide you and that His voice will never lead you astray. Even now, I can hear my Grandma's voice in prayer, "God, You said in Your word 'I am the head and not the tail,' 'I will have more than enough,' and 'You will rejoice to see me do well...'"

*Cultivate a lifestyle of prayer and worship, and see if God won't speak to you.*

## JOURNAL ENTRY: HABIT OF OBEDIENCE

*Proverbs 28:9 NLT "God detest the prayers of a person who ignores the law."*

"Stop praying for stuff and change when you refuse to obey His commands to you. The change is in obedience. Why pray to a God you won't listen to? Since you only listen to yourself, why not pray to yourself? BECAUSE YOU KNOW YOU ARE NOT GOD! HE IS NOT A HUMAN WHO OFFERS ADVICE, HE IS GOD AND HE GIVES INSTRUCTIONS because He knows who He is. Obey His instructions and your prayers won't be drowned in the arrogance of your refusal to submit to His leading. God wants no part of your self-exaltation except to humble you and show you the truth about your position in relation to His.

I wrote this entry in 2013 and re-reading it has blown me away. Obedience is a combination of discipline and faith. This makes me think about the Israelites and how the only difference between the journeys of Egypt, The Wilderness, The Red Sea, and The Promised Land was that each required a new level of obedience and faith. Obedience keeps you on God's ordained path, but faith keeps you obedient. For my personal walk with God, obedience and discipline mean the same thing, because one yields the other. In order to obey God, you not only need faith, you must make daily decisions that will result in the completion of your assignment.

When God sees that you are continually obedient to Him, even to your own discomfort and maybe your emotional hurt, you begin to experience a level of abundance others will not understand. The habit of obedience will cause you to reap abundant joy and peace, not because you're simply happy to obey but because you know your obedience gives God great glory. So when the things around you begin to shake and others shake with it, you are firm in your peace that Christ died for you to have.

Disobedience is one of the heaviest burdens breaking Christians, because refusal to honor God's Word speaks to a hardness toward the Holy Spirit. I've said before that delayed obedience is still disobedience; what God requires of you in this season needs to be started and completed in this season because He has to be in it for you to win at it. **God requires your obedience, not your courage.** Therefore, courage or no courage, you need to stand on His Word that He has not given you the spirit of fear, but of power, love, and a sound mind (1 Timothy 1:7). What does that mean? It means you have the power to honor Him in the way He instructs, and you have the responsive love inside of you that desires to please Him and lead others to Him. It also means you have the discipline to make it even plainer, and to complete every task God requires of you. Further, it means that you have the peace to know that whether man agrees or not, and whether life starts getting crazy or not, "not one good thing will He withhold from those who do His commandments (Psalm 84:11)."

Honestly, sometimes it is a struggle to do what God is asking of you, not because you do not love Him, but because it requires too much emotional control. From 2013-2014, I had a falling out with a family member who was very instrumental in my life after my mother's passing. I decided to retreat from that situation to protect myself from harm by simply staying away from that family member. In staying away, I somehow hurt that person and what should have been a private conversation between the two of us became gossip that was spread among others. When I began to hand the situation over to God and the emotional wreckage that it left behind, He instructed me to go apologize to my family member. Of course, I put it off because I did nothing wrong in my eyes, but in God's eyes I had a chance to show the love of Christ, a chance to demonstrate forgiveness on a level that I did not have to before, and a chance to really prove I trusted Him with all of me. If I truly gave my emotional issues about the situation over to Him and examined myself to see how I was hurtful, then apologizing was the right thing to do. As I delayed in my obedience, the Holy Spirit convicted me through sermons, social media statuses, and even my own thoughts as I laid in bed at night. Disobedience became such a burden to me, and the crazy part is, because Christian disobedience results in conviction from the Holy Spirit, it weighed so heavily on my heart and mind that it grounded me like cement and kept me from moving forward. When I finally obeyed His instruction and apologized, I had such peace within me that I could move forward spiritually.

Although the relationship with my family member has not been mended, my obedience has given me peace, and that obedience has resulted in a different kind of emotional mastery. The surrender of hurtful emotions is difficult. Even though you don't want to feel negative things about the person, sometimes you hold onto them because you know God will not exact revenge for you being offended, but offer them grace and mercy. Beloved, when we are hurt by others, our commission then is not to get revenge, but to pour out ourselves for Jesus so that others can see Him in us and come to glorify the Father in heaven. When God tells you to go apologize, even though you don't see how you did anything wrong, it gets tough, but you have to ask yourself, is obedience now worse than a hard heart?

As an example of obedience, we can examine the downfall of King David. The very reason King David saw Bathsheba naked and began to spiral into adultery and murder was because he was not where he was supposed to be. He was supposed to be out to battle with the troops, concerned with God's business; the same can happen to any of you and probably has happened to many. The reason you walk so easily into some temptations is because you made room for them by not being where you were supposed to be in obedience.

Beloved we must develop the habit of obedience, we must practice honoring God, because it is not something that is natural to us. Let honoring God be like developing a runner's lifestyle, just as a runner feels *off* when they don't run, we ought to feel *off* when we don't honor God's explicit instructions. We grow so much closer to God when we are intentional about honoring Him, He knows we can be trusted with people, and we learn that we can definitely overcome the persuasion of the flesh. Obedience is about so much more than you and your feelings, people need your example, they want to know it isn't impossible to be a true Christian in these last days. Let's grow!

# GOD BROKE MY HEART

I wanted to end Broke Down Conviction with this particular message because it is a perceived reality that many believers won't admit to. My failure to confess my thoughts would take away others' permission to do the same. So let me be the second of only two people I know to ever admit this: God broke my heart beloved. But, this isn't the time to accuse me of blasphemy or any other offense. Throughout this book I have shared my choices and how the choices of others changed my life, some pushing me away from God and others toward Him. For many years, I fantasized what my life would be like if my mother was a gainfully employed adult with a husband when she gave birth to me. Of all the straws to pull, why did I get the short one? I was born to a teenage mother who struggled with her identity and had all of her children out of wedlock. She worked menial job as a produce manager and struggled to pay the bills. On top of all of that, the end of her days were saturated with the scorn of many friends and some family as they learned about the disease that would soon bring her demise.

Seriously, why did I have to live in a house where all summer we ate 5 for $1.00 high sodium ramen noodles, and $0.50 boxes of higher sodium Kraft dinner and drank 10 for $1.00 packets of Kool-Aid? Why was having a strawberry a luxury at my house? Why did I only have 4 pairs of shoes, and a church dress stained with gum that I had to wear every other Sunday? Why didn't we ever have a phone or vehicle in case of emergencies, why did we not have running water for months? If God really loved me and He was in control of everything, then why did life get to keep beating me down?

Why did God allow me to be a victim of sexual abuse? A child born from generations of sexual and physical abuse. Why couldn't He stop the cycle before it happened to me? Why did God sit on His throne and not stop my step father from molesting me, or the next man, or my cousins? Didn't He know it would make me hate men, and not value sex? I know that He knew. And after all those years of sexual abuse, I was hit with the ultimate blow, my mother's death! MY ONLY ALLY IN THIS WORLD HAD TO DIE TOO? How much more did God want me to bear before thoughts of taking my own life would plague me and became a reality?

I'll be honest – although we went to church many Sundays, my mother was not a Christian before she was on her deathbed. Growing up, no one was there to cultivate a lifestyle of prayer in me, so I rarely prayed. But when I did pray, I prayed for God to let my mother live. I knew He was so powerful; He could do anything. I also knew that "Jesus loved the little children" so my prayer would be more valuable than those of the adults I was surrounded by. I just wanted my mother to live, and I was tired of life being too hard every day. From the age of five I was given too much responsibility – cooking, cleaning, babysitting, wringing out the laundry with my hands, and helping with homework. Yet, for all my trouble, I got to bury my mother at age 13. Even worse, my mom didn't die of an admirable disease like cancer, where people could solemnly say that she "lost her battle" and herald her as a warrior. Instead, my mother died of AIDS, a disease where people would scorn her even in death and then us, highlighting only her perceived promiscuity and then condemning us to follow in her footsteps. For all my troubles, for having my eyes forcibly opened to sex too early, for living without for so long – I got to become an orphan.

As I grew older, I found myself in the midst of family drama, and rejected by those same people time and time again. Later on, my goal to attend grad school – a goal that I thought would bring me happiness and redemption – did not come to fruition within the time frame I set, which led to further disappointment. To make matters worse, I had a miscarriage soon afterwards...the troubles in my life seemed endless. You know, I used to think for all my troubles God should at least drop $1 billion my way. If I was going to keep suffering without time in between to heal from my past pains, then I would need to do it in expensive Christian Louboutin shoes while living in a mansion and flying first class everywhere I went. Well, given that my husband and I still rent our home, we have a car note to pay, and we actually have to save to buy big ticket items, you can tell that the fortune I requested hasn't happened.

Since I am being so honest, let me continue – I wanted God to feel guilty for the pain inflicted on me by others. I know

He gave man free will, but that same free will that enables me to choose Him, gave opportunity for my pain. I thought that if God truly felt guilty, then He would act like a guilty parent and overcompensate for what I perceived to be His absence, hence me expecting the free $1 billion to fall into my lap. When I was a teenager, I even wrote out a list in my prayer journal of what I would do with the money He'd give me (and yes, I was a saved teenager doing all of this). Yes, I went to church every day of the week and was active in ministry. Yes, I spoke in tongues and would fall out during a powerful worship session. And yes, I was praying for hours with passion like the elders and evangelists. But God was a genie to me, and I expected to get what I asked as reparations for my suffering.

What fed this "God owes me" complex I developed was the fact that He began to bless me "beyond anything I could ask or think." Finally, after years of suffering throughout my childhood, I began to receive. The first of these tremendous blessings was an all-expense paid trip to Madrid, Spain for summer school. Then, as a high school student, I was provided the opportunity to take Spanish courses at the College of the Bahamas. I received a scholarship to attend private school, and my teachers quickly invested their time and resources into me like I was stock guaranteed to deliver a large return. Even my young love life seemed to be flourishing with minimal effort on my part. At the time, I had a boyfriend but never let him hold my hands or kiss me, and yet he did not object to my rules. He was also okay with us never talking about sex – because there was no way it was going to happen! During my high school years, I lived in a home with a married couple who loved Jesus and who showed me what a real-life model of Christian family life should be (thanks Aunty and Uncle). As I continued to grow and reap these blessings, everyone that met me heavily favored me. As icing on the cake, I even had my own bedroom and didn't have to lock the door because I knew that no one was coming in to violate me in any way. God was giving me everything I ever wanted as a teen and young adult.

I know you must be wondering, did I just nullify everything I have said in this section before now and what I will say after? No! Beloved, I admit to God breaking my heart because that was a truth that hindered my walk with Him, and as a result I could not wrap my head around my suffering and immense pain. Losing my mother, losing my siblings, losing my innocence, losing myself, losing my baby – how much loss could one person handle before they wanted to lose their life? In my mind God broke my heart, but in reality He was the only One who could fix what other broken hearts had done to me. All of my pain and suffering was necessary to build up to this moment – this moment when I can confidently say that God loves me, and I know it and I believe it and I walk in it! I know that He reverse-engineered my life story from its conclusion to ensure that none of that pain would kill me, to design my victory in this very moment.

So if you're like me and you feel that God broke your heart at some moment in your past or at the present, I want to tell you that you are not alone in that perception; but your reality tells a different story. Reality shows that we had the displeasure of being heartbroken by others, but we now have the opportunity to experience the privilege of God's great love toward us as He mends our broken hearts. I had to learn that God doesn't owe me anything, but He has purposed to give me everything that matters. Beloved, despite your broken heart, He has engineered this journey so that you can find the confession, clarity, community and opportunity that you seek.

It can be so easy to blame God for not taking the pain away, but in these moments I reminded of John 9:3b "but this happened so the works of God might be displayed in Him." This is the perfect opportunity for the works of God to be displayed in you. Know that the enemy used the authority given to others to inflict what seemed to be unhealable wounds, demonic spirits of rape, molestation, neglect, physical abuse, hopelessness and illness were assigned to your family to make you believe that God doesn't care about you and that your life is worthless. Not so beloved! Our past and present troubles pale in comparison to the coming glory that will be revealed in us (Rom 8:18), and nothing can separate us from His love (Rom 8:38). God is with you and He is for you. Don't let the past become louder than His voice. Refuse to allow anything to turn your head away from the waiting embrace of His love.

Come and be healed.

# 6

# BECOMING NEW

# REDEEMED

This is a journal entry that I wrote while sitting on my Grandmother's bathroom floor in 2013, as I was searching for myself and forced to confront the shameful things I locked away in the rooms of my heart that I kept Jesus out of:

*Dear God,*

*I'm so broken by the secret shame of my choices, what makes it worse is that I don't even regret it. I regret that I hurt You, I believe that I put an irreparable tear in our relationship, a tear not even Jesus' stripes could heal. You must hate me, You* have to! I made the deliberate choice to run away from the consequences of my actions?

I don't know if You can understand, but I didn't want to disappoint anyone. I wanted to protect my family from my humanity. Gosh I don't know if I could ever stomach the piercing stares or the hammering of their disappointing words, surely the only way to make that work would have been to cut everyone in my family off. That wasn't going to work.

I'm afraid. I'm afraid to call You Father again because gosh I know that would cement the disappointment I perceive You feel toward me in hopelessness. How could I call You Father? How could I pray to You again without being punished? You have to punish me God! I've earned this punishment and I just know that I am going to mess up again! Maybe not on this scale, but if You let me burn myself maybe the taste for rebellion will be snuffed out. How could You love me? I don't even love myself! How could You keep caring, do You still care?

I know I prayed the prayer of repentance over and over, I long to repent like my lungs long for oxygen. But no matter how many times I say the words "God please forgive me", I find myself garnishing those same words with "but I had to do it, I couldn't have a baby". I keep reliving the moment my doctor told me I would struggle with fertility, I remember those tears and I felt those aches deep in my womb. I can't help but wonder if those words made me feel free to have sex as I please. Or did they make me defile the sanctity of the bodily communion that is sex over and over again? Either way, I woke up one day and realized my clothes weren't fitting, and the smaller my clothes got the more I thought my life was over. You must think I'm crazy, trying to reason with You about why I had an abortion. There it is....

*Abortion.*

*Abortion.*

*Abortion.*

*Maybe the more I write it the less it will sting, the less these tears will flow down my face, the less I will ache! I'm a Christian, how did I end up on the abortion table? How did I find myself calling my sisters and best friend to tell them, that I – the one who was constantly praying for them and singing in the church choir – was pregnant? How did I get from passionately pursuing You to being lost in a circus of sin and shame?*

*All I remember thinking is that my mother must be rolling in her grave. At 16 years old she had the courage to give birth to me, and at 17 she had the courage to have my brother and accepted she would be talked about and looked down upon because of her choice to have sex. But me? I was a punk! I was a coward! I have no right to mercy! The doctor gave me a report of barrenness and yet my womb was opened when I was most unprepared. What was I supposed to do with a child? Six weeks into the creation process had passed and it took me just 24 hours to decide that I would sacrifice this life for the greater good because I couldn't be like my mother. But there was no greater good was there? It wasn't the baby that I didn't want – it was the shame, the setback, and the failure that I didn't have the courage to face.*

*God, did it break Your heart when I was crying out loud for forgiveness? Did Jesus die for these kinds of sins too? Did He die for my selfishness, my cowardice? Could His blood blot out these sins too? What kind of price will I have to pay God? Maybe if Jesus and I put our money together, it will be enough to cover the cost? Right?*

*My heart aches, my whole soul aches; I've never felt the pain of choosing the "lesser" of two evils. This kind of hopelessness feels like an attractive death; can I recover from such a fall? Has anyone like me been redeemed? Restored?*

*You reap what you sow, right? When my mother planted seeds of irresponsibility, she harvested three unplanned pregnancies, HIV, and then death. I've planted the same seeds, despite her example...surely worse must be in store for me. What will it be God? Cancer? My siblings die and I be left alone? I'll never have love? How can I make it up to You God? I want to make it right! I want to earn Your trust back! I'm not fit for use, I'm a filthy temple, but would You let me try to make it up to You?*

*God please forgive me and help me to forgive myself!*

Beloved, I am sitting here in tears because I carried this burden of shame with me for four years. I got over my foolish desire to earn God's forgiveness so that I could breathe, finally exhaling my hurt and inhaling His grace and embrace of love. But I still struggled with the shame of having an abortion, I know this because I have erased these pages twice, even though God told me to be completely transparent. A war waged within because on one hand, I have been restored and I walk in forgiveness not only from God, but also from myself. However, on the other those closest to us often have trouble moving beyond our truths to a place of acceptance. My family will require answers, but I do not want to answer any questions, as they will attempt to decipher who I was involved with when this all happened. But I know that those questions will come. Even though we have alcoholics and drug addicts in our family who are accepted without judgment, I know the news of my past abortion may entice some to be disappointed in me, while others celebrate with me the great honor of freedom in Christ. How do I, even in my freedom, not allow myself to be bound by my loved ones' responses?

But let's not get off track – this isn't about abortions or even what the Bible says or doesn't say about them. This testimony is about how the deepest pain of my existence made me reject Christ's love. How do you live with yourself after doing something you perceive is unforgiveable in the eyes of the God you say you love? My actions hadn't hurt any one human except myself, and I coped by perfecting my acting skills and faking my happiness as I tried to carry on life as usual. I learned the burden of attempting to make God a victim of my choices. I always knew that the Bible said "Thou shalt not fornicate", but that didn't keep me from doing it time and time again. I was convinced that something was wrong with me. Why was I constantly doing the wrong I didn't want to do? What was added to my life, but pain and sorrow, by fornicating and getting pregnant? I pray your heart sees where I am going with this.

Beloved, I tried to negotiable a hell for myself with God. I was fully convinced of my hopelessness and wanted God to know that I didn't deserve His love. I set out to tell Him not to waste Christ's blood on my sins, on my past, because even though we all were unworthy, I was most unworthy. But the truth is, while I was being knit together in my mother's womb,

God had already reverse-engineered my path. Each grain of dirt, each pebble, each molecule along the way was saturated with redeeming love and grace. Even before the world began, He saw my yearning to be punished with isolation, and yet He extended to me more love and more grace by giving me people to cover my sin and wipe away my shame. I've said it before and I will say it again – all of my pain and shame have come full circle, they have been repurposed for this moment, and God has not wasted any of who I was in making me who I am.

On November 9th of 2016, I found out I was pregnant once again. My husband was fast asleep and I snuck out of bed so as not to awake him. I ran to the bathroom and took my last pregnancy test, telling myself "Shonda it won't be positive, brace yourself, don't cry, don't question God, just accept that it won't be positive." I had already lost one pregnancy and still cried in secret about it, yet here I was nervously excited to know if my body had dared begin creating life once again. Within five seconds, the plus sign showed up on the test. I ran from the bathroom holding in my scream, I opened the front door to the house at 11pm at night and ran into the streets! When I finally stopped running, I began shaking uncontrollably, too emotional to keep the news bottled up inside of me. I called my Aunt Paige all the way in the Bahamas and together we let out a praise from the deepest parts of ourselves. All Aunty Paige knew was that I was told at 19 that I couldn't have a baby, and later on she learned of my miscarriage. I never revealed my abortion to her, or the emotional struggles I experienced.

Throughout my pregnancy I struggled with paranoia, which clouded my thoughts with dangerous questions. Was this gift of life going to be snatched from me? Would I have to push out a dead baby like others I know? Would I die in labor? Will the other shoe from the most painful time of my life drop now, at the happiest time of my life? Would God take this baby away from me because I rejected my unexpected pregnancy? So many times I revealed to God in prayer than I wanted to keep this baby that I had fallen in love with. Isn't it funny how even though we serve God and acknowledge that His ways are not our ways, once we find ourselves struggling with forgiveness we interact with Him like His love is conditional? Like His forgiveness comes with a punishment so that His trust can be regained? It is easy to make a man out of God when you're in a place of spiritual insecurity.

I made it through nine entire months of pregnancy, writing prayers daily for my baby, with my Aunt Paige interceding for me without even knowing I was still battling my past. In the midst of this heated internal battle, I was also writing to you beloved. Presently, my baby boy is here and he's brought with him an unimaginable joy. He gets to have me for a mother and I am blessed to have him as my son, and I am ever so thankful. I guess what I want to say to you here beloved is that your case is never too hopeless for God, you are never unwanted or unloved. You see, that's how His love works – we can never earn it and nothing we can ever do will separate us from it. God's love was with me on the abortion table, His love was with me in the depths of my spiritual depression, God's love was with me when my only companion was the debris of my broken life.

Sometimes, our conviction gets broken because we only want God to keep us from physical harm and danger, but forget that He has already seen all the ripples our actions will have. You see beloved, we were created to be loved and to love. This love manifests in many forms throughout our lives, but every day it manifests itself as protection from ourselves. I was a fornicating Christian resisting protection. When we stop surrendering to the protection of that love, we end up on abortion tables, not just aborting physical fetuses but emotional and spiritual ones as well. If you're like me, you take the long way around back to where you think Jesus is and you delay purpose and break promises to yourself. The problem with breaking the promises you made to yourself is that you delay those around you waiting on the fruit and example of that promise being fulfilled. Furthermore, you start to become numb to conviction.

Beloved, no matter what you have done, God truly is love. Sometimes we cannot understand that love until we perceive ourselves unredeemable, during those desperate moments when we are about to jump off the cliff of life into spiritual suicide. Even when your conviction is broken and you find yourself at prayer meeting on Wednesday, but right back to fornicating on Saturday, His grace remains sufficient and His plan is always redemption. Our selfish decisions and poor choices, our rejection of God's love in those moments of rebellion have been nailed to the cross of Calvary. Our Christ bore them in His body and was separated from His Father so that we could be united with the Father. I love you beloved, come on out of that despair, because as far as you try to run to hide yourself with the fig leaves of work, family, hobbies, TV, and social media, God is looking for you to restore you in His love. Come be redeemed!

# COME AS YOU ARE

My own Broke Down life as a Christian started long before I was even saved. My entire childhood life had been full of mess, defeat, lies, abuse, hatred, sin, and unforgiveness. You see, I was born to teenage parents who were themselves born to teenage parents. My mother contracted HIV from a man who was aware of his status, and knowingly engaged in unprotected relations with her. I remember being told about the day she found out as though it were yesterday. In dazed confusion all she could ask was, "How could you do this to me?" My grandmother went with my mom to the hospital to begin a treatment regimen, but my mother's shame and guilt weighed her down so heavy that each moment in the waiting room waiting for her name to be called, cementing her in the reality of her HIV-positive status, catapulted her right back out the door. In our small Nassau town there was no such thing as having *the ting* (HIV) and keeping it confidential. She fled from treatment and therefore fled from life. So, there she was – HIV-positive, no medicine, with three children, no parental support, and too young to know what to do with the hand she was dealt and the one she chose.

When I was six or seven years old I was retrieved from the outer islands of the Bahamas after living with my grandmother for a short while, only to find my mother living with a psycho, Cam. The walls of our one-bedroom apartment held many painful tales of abuse that no amount of paint or wallpaper could cover up. A moment from 1996 is still vividly ingrained into my memory. As my brother and I pretended to be asleep on the floor, all we could hear was Cam beating our mother like she was his unruly child. I remember her screaming so loudly begging for help and calling out to me saying "Shonda call da' police! Call da' police!" I was so terrified for her life back then, and the way she screamed my name still haunts me to this day. I just knew I had to rescue my mom.

Wearing only an undershirt and panties, I ran out of the apartment and down the street to the local convenience store. In a panic and out of breath, I pleaded with the storeowner, "Mr. Bowe, help pleaz, he beatin' my mummy, call da police. Call da police!" Very coldly, Mr. Bowe asked me if I had a quarter to use the phone, and of course I did not. He was unmoved by my panic, that quarter meant more to him than a child's peace or my mother's safety. I walked out of his store with my head hung low, afraid that I would find my mother dead. When I returned to the apartment, help still hadn't come, but I know that all of my neighbors heard the commotion; they were willing to let my mother die. My mother was sitting on the couch crying while holding my brother. Seeing the anguish and deep sorrow in her eyes, I reluctantly told her what happened at the store and she just held us both and cried. She made a remark about Cam being crazy, and as though he were listening in at the room door, he quickly came out and threw a figurine at my mother that broke on impact with her body. This event marked the downward spiral that became my life back then.

When my mother finally worked up the guts to leave Cam, we moved in with her male friend named Pat, who thankfully only wanted to help a single mother without requiring her body. My mom, due to her enticing physique and rotund bottom, of course garnered many male friends who she called on to look-in on us while she worked two jobs. Among them was Cassius, who was very good at making sure my siblings and I kept our school uniforms clean and had dinner in our bellies. Over time, it became clear that Cassius got tired of working without pay and wanted other compensation. When I was 8 years old, he asked me if I wanted to see a magic trick, and told me he could make milk spout from his body. In reality, his trick violated my innocence, and led me into our kitchen where he sexually abused me. I hate that when I close my eyes, I can still see that moment. Cassius had the disgusting pleasure of abusing me once again before my mother got a boyfriend who soon became her husband and we moved away.

I was so excited to have a father figure, as my own father had not been very active in my life at that time and lived in another country. I was looking forward to a father's present and active love, but what I got instead was the devil's perverted version of a parent-child relationship. OB is what we will call my step-father, who is now deceased. Almost like it was yesterday, I remember the first time he came into our room. We lived in a two-bedroom apartment then and I shared a bedroom with my brother and a bed with my sister. I thought he was coming to check on us like fathers on television did, to tuck us in and kiss us good night. But I was wrongly mistaken. I was an insomniac at the time and struggled to sleep through the night. Each time he entered, I would have to pretend to be asleep, thinking he was going away in a minute – but he stayed, and he molested me. I learned the hard way that the devil has perverted everything that God created to represent relationship with Him in the natural realm, family and intimacy.

He would enter our room night after night, and I tried to hide behind my brother convinced that because he was a homophobic Jamaican man, there was no way he would risk touching my brother in any way before he reached me, but he still got to me. Short of telling my mom the truth, I did everything I could to hinder his pursuits. I would wear two sets of tights and a pair of jean shorts, and lay with my legs tightly interlocked to keep him away. Yet, the small, elementary school girl that I was, was still too weak. I felt so dirty. Every day I had to get up and look in his face, sit at the table with him and ride in his truck like life was normal. He would call me his daughter but he treated me like a prostitute. I desperately wanted to tell my mother but I could not stand the thought of breaking up her happy home. She seemed happy.

One day, while my mother and I watched a Lifetime movie about sexual abuse, she blatantly asked me if anyone had ever touched me inappropriately or tried to molest me, and I lied and said no, thinking I was protecting her. A few weeks later, OB got mad at my mother for something and busted her lip open with a punch to the face. In that moment, I realized that maybe she wasn't as happy as I thought and now would be the time to tell. God truly worked in mysterious ways. In the days to follow, that same Lifetime movie came back on and my mother and I were again watching it together and she asked me, "Shonda anyone ever touch you or molest you?" Finally, I admitted that it was her husband. I think she was in a state of shock and embarrassment, and I can only imagine how she beat herself up over making another foolish relationship decision and not being able to discern a man with worth from an imposter. We went to the police and I was removed from my home and told to go stay with my Aunt. I couldn't believe it, I was the victim but yet I had to leave while the abuser was free to roam and stay in the home with my other siblings. That was not what happened on that Lifetime movie!

My stepdad said that I was making it up, that he never touched me. The police kept grilling me, unconvinced of my story:

"How did you know it was him getting up late at night?" they questioned.

"Because I know, I don't sleep at night, and only he pees that loud."

"You know it's him by the sound of his pee?" they asked annoyed by my lack of evidence.

"Yes, only a man would pee that loud because he has to stand up."

"You sure?"

The police did not believe me so what did my confession

matter anyways?

While I was still staying with my aunt, I got to enjoy the peace of a secure home. One weekday while heading to her place from school, an unknown lady stopped me to tell me about the love of Jesus and how I could be saved. I was nine then but I understood perfectly what she meant. Without hesitation, I decided to give my life to Jesus, and in that same moment, I was asked to say that I lied about being molested by OB so I could come home. I vehemently retorted, "I cannot lie, I am a Christian now!" But, I also wanted to go home, I missed my mother and the police did not believe me and they did nothing to bring me justice. So, I told the agency I wanted to go home, that I didn't think I remembered correctly. Telling that lie filled me with such sorrow. When I got back home OB didn't touch me for a week, and so I thought things had changed, but they didn't. He started back again, he came and asked me one night if he could lay next to me, I told him no. He did so anyway. He wanted to hold me, and apologize for whatever I think he did to me. I was disgusted. I am still disgusted.

I think my mother stopped trusting him because she would come and sleep in front of me and sing to me, and every night that she did that, he would come in and *WHAP!* her with the belt Bahamian children feared greatly, the Land belt and drag her across the tile floor back into their bedroom. It felt as if our little dysfunctional family thrived on destruction, like we couldn't escape it and there was no protecting any of us from our own lies and bad choices. The months that followed found us with no running water, behind on the rent, and OB back to Jamaica to be with his pregnant sidepiece. The problem with him leaving was that he took my mother's $3000 life savings that she planned on investing into a triplex for her children.

Mommy always talked about wanting to leave us something, and I didn't understand why she said those things until one night when I was 11 years old.

My mommy called me into her room and said, "Shonda, I have something to tell you, but you can't tell anyone." I was so excited that she was telling me a secret, it meant she trusted me, but I had no idea that I was about to hear words that would change my life forever.

"You hear me? I say you can't tell anyone," my mother told me.

"Okay mummy, I ga keep da secret, jus' tell me please," I responded in excited anticipation.

"I have AIDS...You hear me? I have AIDS."

Even as I write, my heart sinks into my stomach...I remember it like it was yesterday, I laughed at her to her face. I knew what AIDS was, and there was no way my gorgeous mother with her beautiful shape was living with AIDS. There was no way! How could she have a butt that big and have AIDS? I never even saw her with a flu or fever.

"Mummy you serious?" I asked, shocked.

"Yes, don't tell no one."

That conversation was the last we ever spoke of it. The next day, I went to my 8th grade class and waited until lunchtime to tell someone. There was no way that I could carry that burden by myself at age 11, I knew better than that. My best friend San and I went all the way to the back of the playing field and I told her my mommy was dying of AIDS.

My mother was an abused woman, born to an abused woman, and I was certain to follow that pattern. It was like my family had a genetic abnormality that made us prone to abuse. The only thing we seemed to attract was dysfunction. I cannot even begin to recount the many sleepless nights I spent at age 11, 12, 13, and the rest of my teenage life pondering if I was HIV-positive. I mean, I had to be, just as simple as $1 + 1 = 2$. It meant that OB + Mommy + me molested by OB = me with HIV.

On my first day of 9$^{th}$ grade, years after OB had left, my mom decided she needed to go to the hospital because she felt her heart murmuring. I had already put behind me that she was HIV-positive, and stigmas of her illness no longer bothered me. I drank from every cup she had, ate with her fork if I had to, and took bites from her sandwiches. We carried on with life as normal as we could. When I came home from school that day, I heard her weeping uncontrollably and I found a makeshift will written on a scrap of paper describing how to divide the five pieces of jewelry, a television and her clothes amongst her children. When I finally spoke to her, she said the doctor told her she had Stage 4 AIDS and six months to live. I could see the defeat in her eyes, she had surrendered to death. After all, it was her only ally by then. I could see the defeat as she held the will realizing she had nothing to show for her life's suffering except three soon-to-be orphaned children and five pieces of jewelry. She never owned a car or a house, lost her life savings to a worthless husband, never had a healthy relationship with a man or herself, and spent her days struggling to make ends meet.

Don't get me wrong, my mother was one of the kindest people I knew – she gave what she didn't have, she was there for everyone, and always put others above herself. Each day before I left for school, she would tell me to go conquer the world and be better than she was. I can remember her saying, "Shonda, I ene nuttin' and it might be too late for me to be someting, but you go be somebody baby!" She pushed me mercilessly to excel in school, and discouraged me from giving into peer pressure of any kind. She never hid her poor choices from me by pretending to have been perfect or that her current choices were right. I knew each and every day that she loved me deeply. She worked hard to provide and did whatever it took to survive the boxing match she was in with life.

By October 2004 my siblings and I were called into the hospital to visit our mother who, according to the doctor, was "on her way out". In the hospital, I watched as her voluptuous wide hips and big butt withered down to nothing. I remember her sitting down in the visitors' section with a large bowl of vomit in her hands, because she could no longer keep her food or medication down. I didn't understand that she was dying, and I hated myself because I didn't take that chance to tell her what she meant to me. The last time I saw her alive, she was wearing a diaper and connected to a dialysis machine. I could smell her body rotting, she smelled like death. It took 10 minutes for her to work up the energy to utter the words "Shonda I love you". She was so far gone... it was then that I realized she was never coming home. In the minutes right before her death, she had one final moment of clarity during which she said that she wanted to know Jesus, and she wanted to see the scriptures. After accepting Christ, she planned her funeral and decided who her children would live with.

On November 6, 2004, I was woken out of my sleep by my grandmother telling me she was going to the hospital. When she left the house, a voice in my head said, "Mummy dead," and the sunrise brought confirmation. My 30-year-old mother was dead, and me? I was officially an orphan. I felt like death had overcome me too, I wanted to lay down and die alongside her. I needed to die to escape the hurt and the emptiness. I was so ashamed that my mother died of AIDS, I told everyone who asked about her cause of death that she had bad kidneys. My self-hatred and anger grew every time I saw the man that infected her living his life and smiling freely. I hated him more and more with each passing day. I hated my mother for the way she lived her life, I ruminated over her decisions and thought if she had just made a wiser decision, then maybe she would be here today and I would not be alone.

Life had officially destroyed us both, her body was dead but I was left alive to feel all of the pain. It was like anesthesia awareness: undergoing surgery, paralyzed by anesthesia, yet awake and unable to scream out and say that I could feel all the searing pain. There was no hope for me; I knew I was bound to the same stupid, destructive chaos that swept my mother away...

Or so I thought!

This book, Broke Down Christians, is not about me fixing you, but about understanding the power of surrender, and choosing what battles we will enter in this life. I never needed to fight against my past, but I needed to surrender to my God-ordained future. I never needed to try and fix myself, I only needed to surrender to the love and Word of God as my awareness of them grew. I got saved at age 13, on November 14, 2004, the day we buried my mother, and I have struggled to be a whole Christian since then. I have fornicated, I have lied, I have gossiped, I have judged, I have hated, I have been mean, jealous and envious, I have stolen things, I have deceived people, I have cheated God, I have backslidden over and over again, and I have made people feel hopeless. I have abused the mercy of God, and today even this book comes after the sin of procrastination. I am not counting my sins, for I know that I have been forgiven, Praise God. But instead, I present myself to you as vulnerable as I know how, because I dare to show you the great love Jesus has for me, a Broke Down Christian. He loves me so much that He trusts me with a message to you, and that love is so enduring that it never left me in any of the pits I dug for myself or the graves that others dug for me. You see beloved, being a Broke Down Christian is not about counting your sins, it's about recognizing that not even those horrible, dirty stains of sin can separate us from God's love and outreach. We just need to reach back for Him in return. We just need to turn our face away from our own shame and complacency, to see the liberty in His embrace.

Many days, I thought I was beyond God's reach, only to now realize that He knew about these self-destructive habits even before I was given life. Before the world began, He saw the depression and suicidal thoughts that would result from my mother's death and deliberate sins. He saw me being molested and becoming full of hatred and rage and knew I would need peace and freedom. He saw my poverty and knew it would birth envy, and that I would need contentment. He saw my pride and knew I would need humility. And despite all of this, He still said, "I will go down and redeem LaShonda for Myself, I will show her she is not too dirty for Me to love extravagantly. I will love her back to me. I will show her she is capable of love and beauty and joy. I will show her that there is purpose for her brokenness." I believe He says the same about all of us.

It is perfectly okay that you are broken down right now, but what's not okay is that tomorrow finds you in the same stagnant and ineffective condition as a Christian. Take a moment to picture with me a broken down car on the side of the road. In that state, a broken down car is useful for nothing more than being picked apart for scrap metal to become parts of other cars' restoration. A broken down vehicle cannot fulfill its purpose of moving from point A to point B. It cannot travel, provide AC in the hot summers or heat in the cold winter, and if it stays in the open it will rust and continue to deteriorate. The same thing happens to us when we choose to stay broken down – we are ineffective in the cause of Christ, and our concept of Christ and relationship with Him begin to rust. He loves us so extravagantly that our surrender to that love makes us whole, keeps us, revives us, and enables us to be conduits of His great love. I sit here in tears because I can genuinely see with my heart's eye, the heart of God towards us. I can see how He wants to use us and keep us faithful to Him instead of our lives being a cycle of backsliding and repenting that comes from making the same immature decisions and having a heart divided between Christ and the world.

Beloved, you don't have to live like Christ's love is ineffective, like His grace isn't sufficient. Even though you will do wrong, you don't have to live in a cycle of backsliding that taints your witness of Christ. At the end of it all, I want my pain to count as purpose, and to this end it has. I want my life to have been poured out as an offering to God, I want to be the evidence that God is still operating in the lives of human beings on a very intimate level, and I want the same for you. Despite my daily struggles to die to self, take up my cross and follow

Christ all 24 hours of each day, my genuine earnest desire is to advance the name of Jesus Christ. At the end of my life, I do not want to be afraid to die, but excited to rest from time because I know it would mean I have reached eternity, where I will reign with Him. I would have finished the race and Jesus will announce my new name in heaven declaring that I am truly His. Just like you, I have choices to make. I can either choose to live with my eyes, heart, and mind fixed on eternity, running this race to win and storing up treasures in heaven through pure motives and service. Or, I live a selfish life that earns me much wealth, human connections, and travel experiences, but stand before Christ empty and rejected.

I wanted to offer you confession, clarity, and community. I have confessed to inspire your confession. I have shared the clarity I have been given through my healing and refining. Now we have community, not to be miserable together, but to spur each other on in this journey toward the mark of the high calling in Christ Jesus. So come as you are, broken, immature, ineffective, hurting, procrastinating... and be transformed, be healed.

# A PRAYER FOR US

Dear Jesus,

Thank You! Thank You for Your great love and kindness. Thank You for Your mercy, how You love us so deeply and perfectly in our states of imperfection that we can never understand. You are oxygen Jesus, when we are drowning in life's ocean. You are a parachute, when we have stopped acting like Eagles and are diving for the ground. You are the bungee cord when we willingly jump off the safe place. You oh Jesus are the very ventilator when we are in a coma, the very cast on our broken spiritual bodies as we drag around life, the oxygen tank we carry around because we can barely breathe. Thank You Jesus for Your love. Help us to recognize it! Help us to recognize You Jesus Christ! Help us to recognize Your embrace. And please grant us a Hosea 2:14-16 & 19-20 experience:

"But then I will win her back once again.

I will lead her into the desert

and speak tenderly to her there.

I will return her vineyards to her

and transform the Valley of Trouble into a gateway of hope.

She will give herself to me there,

as she did long ago when she was young,

when I freed her from her captivity in Egypt.

When that day comes," says the Lord,

"you will call me 'my husband'

instead of 'my master.'"

I will make you my wife forever,

showing you righteousness and justice,

unfailing love and compassion.

I will be faithful to you and make you mine,

and you will finally know me as the Lord.

Turn our hearts back to You oh God, that we may respond to Your great love by living a life of love. Thank you that a life of love means maturity, honesty, integrity, service, selflessness, graciousness, gratitude, humility, joy, meekness and peace. Lord, in one or many ways, we are broke down Christians and we are in need of You, please make haste to help us... we want to be better.

In Jesus' Name we pray,

Amen.

# BROKE DOWN CHRISTIANS

## ABOUT THE AUTHOR

An outgoing and outspoken native of Nassau, Bahamas, LaShonda enjoys Bible study, travel, photography and writing. She came to the USA in 2009 to pursue a Bachelor of Arts in Interdisciplinary Studies with a concentration in Public Health. During that time she has studied in three countries, and traveled to seven. LaShonda has served in several organizations and was intensely committed to highlighting the condition of drug rehabilitation facilities in the metro Richmond, VA area for two years. Currently, LaShonda works as an Administrative Assistant for a brokerage of life insurance agents and serves by coaching others in areas of Bible study techniques and prayers. Most of all she is enjoying her new baby boy, while attending graduate school to earn a Master of Health Science. LaShonda's further writings can be found at canyourdryboneslive.com where she blogs to empower Christians to study the Word of God.

www.ingramcontent.com/pod-product-compliance
Lightning Source LLC
LaVergne TN
LVHW051054080426
835508LV00019B/1874